Insight:

Reflections on the Gifts of Being an Introvert

Beth L. Buelow

For Andy, my favorite introvert.
I love you.

CONTENTS

Author's Note   i

Part One: What It Means to be an Introvert

1   The Secret Life Of Introverts   4

2   Can We Stop with the "Introvert=Shy" Already?   7

3   I Am Introvert, Hear Me Roar!   12

4   You Wanna Piece of Me? The Fierce Introvert   15

5   No Introversion, Denied!   20

6   Rise of the Introvert   23

7   Speaking Introvert: Becoming Personality Bilingual   27

8   Can Being an Introvert Help You Overcome Shyness?   32

9   Table for One, Please   37

10   7.5 Reasons I'm Grateful to be an Introvert   42

Part Two: Life as an Introvert Entrepreneur

11   You Miss Every Shot You Don't Take   46

12   Quiet Cultivation: Introverts as Leaders   48

13   4 Ways to Keep the Lifeblood From Being Sucked Out of You at Events   53

14   How to Kick Your Analysis by Paralysis Addiction   57

15   The Introvert Entrepreneur or: How I Learned to Stop Worrying and Love the Telephone   61

16   How to Know When Two Heads Would Be Better Than One   66

17   What the Eiffel Tower Teaches Us About Process   72

18   You Must Be Present to Win: Networking for the   75
     Introvert Entrepreneur

Part Three: Miscellanea

19   Weaving in Your Spirit String   80

20   Life Lessons From the Lake   82

21   What to do When You Have a Yucky, Mucky, Sucky Day   85

22   How to Eat an Elephant   88

23   Why "Fake It 'Til You Make It" is Lousy Advice   92

24   How to Stop Thinking and Start Living   96

25   Don't Tell Me to "Step Outside My Comfort Zone"   100

26   What I'll Never Say "Just Do It" Ever Again   103

27   It Really IS a Conspiracy   107

28   You Know You're an Introvert When...   110

     About the Author   115

     Further Reading   117

AUTHOR'S NOTE

My favorite kind of books are those that offer me a bit of inspiration combined with information I can use. They include humor alongside the profound, pragmatism up against imagination.

Above all, they challenge me to see myself and my world differently.

I like bite-sized chapters that allow me to browse and get just the right dose of information before I'm off to the next thing (usually falling asleep!).

That's the idea behind "Insight: Reflections on the Gifts of Being an Introvert." It's a compilation of pieces that speak specifically to the introvert, mixed in with topics that are more general but still interesting to anyone who wants to deepen his or her self-awareness.

My wish for everyone - especially introverts - is that we all live in alignment with our natural energy and strengths.

I hope you find this book an affirming, thought-provoking companion on your journey.

Beth L. Buelow, July 2012

i

Part One:

What It Means to Be an Introvert

To be a soulful person
means to go against all the pervasive,
prove-yourself values of our culture
and instead treasure
what is unique and internal
and valuable in yourself
and your own personal evolution.

-Jean Shinoda Bolen

1| The Secret Life of Introverts

Painfully shy.
Low self-esteem.
No self-confidence.
No social skills.
Afraid of people.
And yes, a loser.

How do I even survive in the world, if this is what people think of introverts!

These were just a few of the words a good friend used to describe an "introvert" when I asked him to define one. He even referred to it as something that may need to be "fixed."

Now, I love my friend dearly. He is incredibly smart, aware and mature. However, on this point, he's completely 110% wrong.

Once I set him straight (and as nice as I can be, I can definitely set someone straight), I recognized that a large part of the reason I feel called to specialize in coaching introverts is because we are a misunderstood, stereotyped bunch. There are stories about introverts –

ones made up by others, ones we make up about ourselves – that can hold us back in a predominantly extroverted world. I wish to empower every introvert I know to understand, own and leverage the gifts and strengths that come with being inwardly focused.

What is an introvert? According to the Jung Lexicon, introversion is "a mode of psychological orientation where the movement of energy is toward the inner world."

So, what does that mean? In simple terms, it means that an introvert is someone who gains energy when alone and drains energy when around too many people.

An introvert can be, as one of my friends puts it, "happy as pie" spending time alone. An extrovert is likely to become bored or lonely after 15 minutes of solitude.

Other introvert traits and preferences include (this is a generalized list; there as many different variations and levels of introversion as there are introverts):

> Think carefully before speaking or acting
> Prefer to express feelings in writing rather than talking
> Excellent listeners
> Have a selected few deep, close friendships
> Dislike small talk
> Enjoy self-reflection and introspection
> Can have different public and private personas

It's that last one that trips people up the most. Anytime I've mentioned I'm an introvert, I almost always hear "No way! I never would have guessed." It's not that I'm a split personality or that what you see in public is not the "real" me. It's simply that over time, I've learned to manage my energy to match the situation. I know how to be super social or spontaneous and still take care of myself and my needs.

All of us, no matter what our orientation, have elements of introversion and extroversion. In my case, it's a dial by which I can turn the volume up or down as I wish, and my dial default is several notches towards introversion.

One point I want to be crystal clear about: claiming the word "introvert" is not about slapping a label on you, or putting you into this little box. It's about having another piece of information that can help you understand yourself better, to help you be true to yourself.

If you're an extrovert, you may be asking, "Hey, what about me? Where's the love?" Rest assured, I love you, too. ;-) My mission as a coach, writer, teacher and personal development fanatic is to facilitate self-understanding and empower people to trust their truth. While I may use the word "introvert" a lot, that doesn't mean that extroverts won't find value, meaning and insight in my message.

2| Can We Stop with the "Introvert=Shy" Already?

Oh dear, did that title sound exasperated? I think it did. Because I am.

Over the past 18 months, I've been especially in tune with articles and posts that mention introversion. And so often, there is a collapsing of the definitions of introvert and shy. The article will start out OK, positing that introverts can be leaders, or business owners, or sales people. Then they will highlight a particular person, first by describing how he or she was shy as a youth. The shyness may be true, and it's somewhat irrelevant to his or her status as an introvert.

As long as I see credible news outlets and bloggers interchange "introvert" with "shy" (or just as inaccurately, with "passive," which is what the Harvard Business Review did in reports of recent leadership research), I know that we need to keep beating the "introvert-does-not-equal-shy" drum.

(Quick note: I am NOT saying there's anything wrong or shameful with being shy. It's simply that as long as we accept incorrect definitions, we'll not have access to the solutions or information that can help us the most. Making an accurate assessment of the situation leads to better solutions.)

The past 12 months have found me in front of more than 25 different groups, for a total audience exceeding 1,500. Each time I speak, I start out by asking people what words or phrases come to mind when they hear the words "introvert" and "extrovert." 100% of the time, "introvert" immediately triggers "shy." Other words that make a regular appearance: quiet, reserved, thoughtful, pensive, contemplative, recharges through alone time, and sexy (sexy? Yes, that one was shouted out at a presentation. When someone mentioned it was true for extroverts, too, I affirmed that yes, anyone who embraces who they are and radiates confidence in it is indeed attractive and sexy!).

Here's what I share about the difference between introvert and shy: Introversion is a personal trait that informs where we gain and drain energy. Introverts gain energy from solitude and quiet, and we drain energy from social interaction. We are internally oriented, most closely in touch with and living from our inner world. We're also likely to be internal processors; we think before we speak, rather than thinking out loud. We live from the inside, out.

I can see why this can be confused with shy. We see someone being quiet, or not approaching people at a party, or squirreling away to work on a project, and we think that person is not comfortable with people, i.e., shy. And that person might very well be shy. Or, he might simply be introverting. (More on that in a second.)

Your typical introvert enjoys people. Human beings are social creatures – we must interact with others. The introvert needs smaller doses of that interaction, most often on his/her own terms. (Planning a surprise party for an introvert? You might want to rethink that.) To have the energy for social interaction, solitude is required.

Shyness means that a person is not at ease in the company of others; easily frightened; timid (World English Dictionary). It's about feeling anxiety about approaching others.

Can an introvert be a shy person? Yes. Can introvert feel shy on occasion? Of course. Can an extrovert be or feel shy? Absolutely!

So an introvert walks into a party (sounds like the start of a joke, doesn't it?). If I'm simply introverting (preserving and pacing my energy), then I'm scoping things out, talking to a few people and slipping away to the restroom or outside so I can take periodic breathers from the activity. I see lots of interesting people in the room. I'm checking things out to see if approaching them is worth the expenditure of energy I know it will require. If I choose not to approach them, it's not out of fear or shyness; it's because I've decided to preserve or expend my energy in an intentional way.

If I'm a shy person at that party, I'm feeling some anxiety and self-consciousness. I want to talk to people, but I feel too much fear to approach them. Or I'm intimidated. Or the pressure is too much. My decision not to approach them isn't so much about choice as it is about anxiety.

To be a shy introvert would be challenging, but in my mind, not as challenging as it would be for the extrovert. The extrovert gains energy from social interaction. If you are a shy extrovert, the anxiety about interaction is at odds with the need for interaction.

Another difference? You can overcome or work through being shy. In most cases, it's desirable to make an effort to do so, if it's showing up in unhealthy ways. You don't "overcome" or "recover" from being an introvert. It's not something to recover from. It's a trait to understand and honor (remember, your sex appeal is at stake here).

I've taken to thinking of introversion less as a personality trait and more of an energetic trait. Does it influence my personality and how I show up in the world? Definitely. But more than that, my introversion dictates my energy sources and suckers. It informs how I relate to the world, from that inside-out place. When we think of personality, we think of sociability (how likable, friendly or social someone is). That's why I think shy and introvert continue to be confused. If we think of introversion as being an energetic – rather than social – trait, we might have a prayer of restoring the word to its original and truer meaning.

Some people think common usage trumps correctness. In other words, if we keep using two words interchangeably and society morphs the meaning, then we should just go along with it. There are times when that's OK (for instance, for the sake of my blood pressure, I've given up on the correctness battle between "more than" and "over."). Other times, it's not acceptable (its vs it's, anyone?). To me, it's critical to bust the introvert=shy common usage. To allow introversion to continue to be equated with shyness (and vice versa) is doing a disservice to people with either trait and keeps us from getting information that would best support us.

I'm not anti-social;
I'm pro-solitude.

-Unknown

3| I Am Introvert, Hear Me Roar!

On May 4, 2010, I announced on my Facebook Fan Page that I was rolling out *a new focus on life and leadership coaching for introverts*. Right out of the gate, a woman asked a question that gets at the heart of why I chose this specialty (actually, it chose me, but that's another story). She shared that she is an introvert then asked, "*What are some tips for becoming more extroverted?*"

The question resonated with me, because I've spent time pondering that myself. My short answer was "I don't advocate for introverts becoming more extroverted; that's working against your natural energy/personality, not with it." And I remembered a blog entry from almost a year ago that spoke exactly to this point. In alignment with Mercury being in retrograde, I'm putting my blog in retrograde to share the entry with you. Enjoy!

May 2009:
Entering into the half-way point of 2009 (already?), I'm reflecting more deeply on a commitment I made at the beginning of the year: ***show up, show up, show up***. The idea of showing up – being present physically, emotionally, spiritually, professionally – felt like a foundational piece of my personal growth strategy. It would support my need to make friends in a relatively new community, as well as be vitally important to building my coaching business.

I did well for much of the first part of the year. Biznik events, a book group, a women's networking event, coach association meetings, masterminds... I showed up to all of them, as completely as I could. My goal of showing up also started to take on a new twist: showing up BIG. Within my network are people who have this magnificent, high energy that draws people to them and holds their attention. I wanted to be like them.

And I set forth that intention several times. For example: I am a magnet that draws people to me; I have energy to spare and share; I am a memorable presence. I thought the key was being more like the people I admired: outgoing, outspoken, just generally OUT.

You can probably guess where I'm heading with this... after working with my coach and lots of conversations with a trusted friend, I realized that *my definition of "big" was based on the way other people were showing up*, rather than what was true for me. I'd defined "big" as high energy. Since I was feeling relatively small, I was low energy. Hmmm... not very coach-like thinking.

Further reflection has brought me to my truth: *that my energy isn't low or high – it is mine.* My unique and positive presence. My energy is calm, attentive, curious and centered. That's what is authentic for me. It's an energy that has its own power and magnetism, no better or worse than an energy that spins visibly faster.

Another truth: I was both inspired and intimidated by people with a more obviously extroverted energy. How could I partner with them? Would I end up in the shadows, or second chair?

What I've discerned is that my energy – and therefore, the way I show up – is a strength, and it's perfect the way it is. *And now I'm aware that I want to fully own it and trust it.* I realize that in a partnership, it's desirable, even necessary, to have that balance, the Yin-Yang.

Therefore, the second half of 2009 will be focused on showing up Big-According-To-Beth. I expect great things to happen.

4| You Wanna Piece of Me?!: The Fierce Introvert

You know how sometimes a word keeps popping up over and over, so much so that you have to stop a moment and wonder why? Over the past few weeks, my word-pop has been "fierce." It's not a word I've used very much, and I've certainly never used to describe myself or anyone I knew.

I mean, really, come on... I'm an introvert!

One of my clients, though, is immersing himself in claiming his fierceness. And I can understand why I've never claimed it for myself. When I right-click on the word, synonyms that I'm offered include "violence," "anger" and "sternness."

But that's not what my client is working on. He's exploring what it means to be fiercely authentic, honest and present. For him, it's about trusting and living according to his highest truth, while being compassionate and open with others. Rather than roll over when others push, or act indifferent just to be the peacemaker, **he wants to fiercely HIMSELF and his truth.**

This has not been without its risks. Because people were used to him being a certain way, his newly-owned fierceness took some by surprise. He may have swung the pendulum too far to the other side; some mistook fierce for harsh. It's natural; when we're trying to adopt a new behavior or belief, we often go to the opposite extreme, so we can eventually land in the middle sweet spot.

At this point, it's interesting to note that he's an extrovert, and he chose the word "fierce" to describe how he wanted to show up. That got me thinking: I never would have voluntarily chosen the word "fierce" for myself... **can a "good girl" who's also an introvert be fierce?**

So I did what we do these days: I took the question to my Facebook community. I asked "What does it mean to be 'fierce'?"

iCathy replied: "**Can you be a gentle personality and be 'fierce'?** There have been times in my life when my strength of convictions made it easy for me to say 'No' (for example). But, there have been times when a 'stronger' personality or subtle pressure influenced me to make a decision I later regretted. Like your client, **I want to own fierceness within myself.**"

Right on! As I reflected on the question and read the Facebook comments, I started to feel a kinship with the word "fierce." I began to see it as another way to describe my passion and conviction, but with an extra edge that made me unstoppable.

Here are more insights my fellow introverts (i) and extroverts (e) shared about the word "fierce":

iJudy: Beth, I see "fierce" as entirely different from "harsh." It's a combination of powerful and passionate. It's ideas you won't let go of because you believe in them so much. And people can have a quiet fierceness and I think that still comes through.

iLori: Fierce doesn't mean cruel or harsh! It means persistent, knowledgeable, valuing customers, doing what it takes to fulfill your customer's needs. You are a force to be reckoned with, but only by your competitors!

iArden: Hmmm, I might use the word conviction. When we have conviction we speak passionately and confidently. We don't have to force it.

eMaria: I love that word....reminds me of Christian from that past Season of Project Runway! MEE—OW

iVal: Fierce honesty and fierce authenticity are lovely goals, unlike harshness. But of course we tend to go through a pendulum swing before finding the middle. It's so worth working on.

A good way to learn that balance is through Non-Violent Communication classes, which helped me a lot. It teaches you assertiveness while staying loving. It helps you understand the connection and practice it in words.

eRachel: In therapy-land, we call that a "change back" reaction. Has your client read "The Dance of Anger"? Cause to me, "fierce" has some of the fire of anger in it, but channeled well and to a purpose.

iKris: Fierce is commitment. Harsh is selfish.

iJames: If your actions are backed by PASSION and positive intentions, then you can be as fierce as you want!

And **iBarry** brought up a famous introvert who's been in the spot light lately. He wrote, "I thought I knew until I saw **Zuckerberg in the Social Network**...I got a long way to go. LOL"

My bottom line: the more I think about it, the more I'm attracted to the word and want to claim a piece of its power for myself.

Being fierce is about being **confident. Passionate. Invested. Intentional. Energetic.** As Judy said, there's a way to have a quiet fierceness that is in harmony with your introvert nature. It's a state of mind, a way of carrying yourself. It's about owning your choices, because they're based in your truth.

And in my personal fierceness, there's abundance. There's no room for scarcity. I want to be so solid in my truth that I can share myself – or people can even take a piece of me – and I won't fear the loss. **I know that I have, and I am, more than enough.**

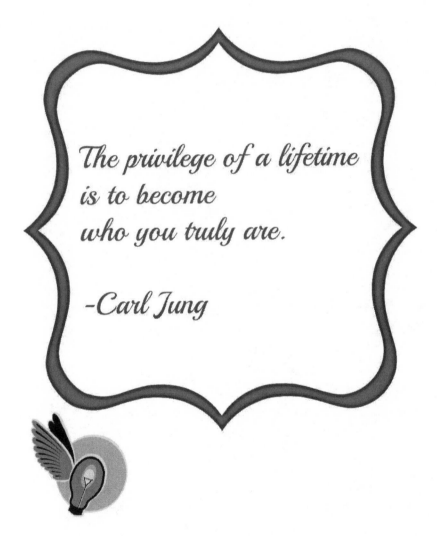

The privilege of a lifetime
is to become
who you truly are.

-Carl Jung

5| No Introversion, Denied!

How often do you find yourself saying, "Part of me wants to this, but another part of me wants to that"? This and that might be stay home or go out, order dessert or "be good," find a new job or stay put. And how often does saying or thinking that way leave you more than a little frustrated?

That internal tug-of-war actually serves a powerful purpose in your life. There are literally parts of you that are giving you information. This isn't about multiple personalities or hearing voices; that's a completely different ballgame. These parts are actually selves, and we have hundreds, if not thousands, of selves bouncing around inside us. Since the mind can't handle all of those voices talking at once (imagine being on the floor of the New York Stock Exchange during trading hours), our psyche has separated them out so that we are in close contact with only a few at a time.

The method for getting in touch with and listening to these selves is called Voice Dialogue. It was developed by psychologists Hal and Sidra Stone in the 1970s, and continues to evolve and be practiced today, by therapists and coaches alike.

A very simple definition offered on their website reads "Voice Dialogue is the basic method for contacting, learning about, and working with the many selves that make up each of us." In a Voice Dialogue session, a facilitator works with the client to bring out different selves for conversation. (This is a very simplistic and limited description of Voice Dialogue; for more information, I highly recommend visiting the websites of Hal and Sidra Stone and The Voice Dialogue Institute.)

A key part of Voice Dialogue is that it's an opportunity to identify and give a voice to our primary and disowned selves. Our primary selves are the ones that come forward when someone asks you, "How would you describe yourself?" and you respond with words such as "responsible, fun-loving, honest, trustworthy, nurturing." Those traits each represent a Primary self. They are how the world sees you, and how you see yourself in the world. These selves emerge relatively early in life, because they are the traits that were affirmed and encouraged by your parents, teachers and friends. These selves keep you safe from rejection or harm; they make sure you are socially acceptable.

On the flip side, disowned selves are the parts of you that were deemed socially unacceptable. These might be the selves who are adventurous, silly, shy, loud, creative, assertive, pessimistic, the drama queen or the class clown. Those same influences that inform the traits that emerge as our primary selves also inform what we disown, through discouraging particular behaviors, expressions or feelings.

And that brings us to the insight I had in the wee small hours of the morning. A few days ago, I read Sophia Dembling's article on the Psychology Today blog, "How to Piss Off an Introvert." She highlights several grievances that she has about how people respond to introverts. One of my favorites, which I've personally experienced on many occasions, is when someone learns I'm an introvert and replies (or exclaims with surprise and dismay), "You're not an introvert!"

What does that have to do with Voice Dialogue? It's an obvious example of how the introverted part of introverts (because we are not 100% introvert) is rejected and disowned by other people. When someone says "You're not an introvert," it's like they're saying, "Being an introvert is not OK. Don't put yourself down like that. You're not one of them." And in fact, they may think that they are paying you a compliment.

Since they disown and reject our introversion, we often disown it as well. The clear message is "it's not safe or acceptable to be introverted." So we go against our nature and try to be extroverted, in order to be more socially acceptable.

The truth? It is natural and acceptable to honor your introverted preferences! What would happen if introverts everywhere developed personal Pride of Ownership? What if we all were secure enough to really own our introvert strengths, our unique and quiet energy?

Part of being able to do that requires taking time to notice and appreciate the gifts our introversion gives us. Voice Dialogue, completing an assessment and coaching are several ways to shine the light on hidden strengths.

The more you understand, own and appreciate your introversion, the more you'll be able to step in to who you truly are. And then, statements like "you're not an introvert!" can roll off you like water off a duck's back, instead of prompting the tempting response Sophia shares, "shut your piehole." :-P

6| Rise of the Introvert

The Sept/Oct 2010 issue of Psychology Today features a cover story by Laurie Helgoe, Ph.D., titled, "Revenge of the Introvert." I've wanted to write about it, because it's an excellent article that brings together scientific research with real life stories of introverts who are acknowledging and honoring their preferences and needs.

Something's been bugging me, though. It's the word "revenge." I know it's a play on "Revenge of the Nerds," and it still bugs me.

According to Dictionary.com, words used to define "revenge" include "vindictive," "retaliation," "vengeance" and "resentful."

Those are some pretty powerful words. And the title doesn't match what I took away from the article.

Square Pegs, Round Holes

Several people quoted in the article – including Helgoe – discovered that they were trying to fit themselves into others' expectations, especially when it came to professional choices. With understanding came compassion, and with compassion came empowerment to work with their preferences (taking smaller case load, forgoing after-work socializing, becoming a solopreneur). They make it clear that by owning their introversion, they can live according to their own rules, rather than the "shoulds" that surround them.

The Island of Misfit Joys

The article shared some fascinating information about happiness, or lack thereof. As Helgoe points out, we end up "feeling less happy, then feeling guilty and inadequate for feeling that way."

This begs the question: what is "happiness"? According to the article, in the United States, people rank "happiness" as their most important goal, and introverts generally don't describe feeling "happy" as a top priority. Perhaps our definition is different. For me, "happiness" is more transitory and circumstantial. And it's not a goal I pursue – it happens to me, often when I least expect it (which makes me happy). I want to create and attract something more sustainable... contentment, freedom, ease and flow. Satisfied with my own definition, I'm able to release myself from any guilt or feelings of inadequacy if my "happiness" looks, feels and sounds different from yours.

It's All Relative

Helgoe mentions the "Big Five" in personality typing: extroversion, neuroticism, agreeableness, conscientiousness and openness. When I first learned of those five traits several months ago, I was annoyed. It was as if psychologists were starting with a measuring stick of extrovert and judging our personality based on that. Helgoe is more objective; she sees the inclusion of extroversion as inferring introversion.

Perhaps this is where the revenge comes in for me, or at least, where I get prickly. I took a quick "Big Five" online assessment. No surprise, I came out at the introverted end of the Extroverted scale. The descriptions for each of the five traits are not unbiased, and maybe they aren't intended to be. Extroversion read: "High scorers tend to be sociable, friendly, fun loving, talkative; Low scorers tend to be introverted, reserved, inhibited, quiet." While the words describing low scores don't offend me too much, they might as well read "not sociable, not friendly, not fun-loving, not talkative." Perhaps I'm being too sensitive; I like to think I'm simply being an inquisitive and reflective introvert.

So, where was I? Oh yeah, "revenge." What I see happening is less revenge and more the start of a reclaiming, a rising up, a celebration of our true essence. There is a movement towards "pride of ownership" in being an introvert as we understand and claim what it really means. And this movement is not what I imagine when I hear the word "revenge" (a word I can't say without crinkling my nose and squinting my eyes in hostility). It's a growing chorus of voices, confident and persistent, writing and speaking out in ways that raise awareness in introverts and extroverts alike.

Be who you want to be...
not what others
want to see.

-Unknown

7| Speaking Introvert: Becoming Personality Bilingual

Calvin: *Sometimes when I'm talking, my words can't keep up with my thoughts. I wonder why we think faster than we speak.*
Hobbes: *Probably so we can think twice.*
~Bill Watterson, *Calvin & Hobbes*

So often in organizations, teams and relationships that have broken down, everyone points the finger of blame in one direction: to communication, or rather, the lack thereof. The exchange between Calvin and Hobbs highlights perfectly why there are so many problems: our thoughts and our speech don't always align in a way that pleases everyone.

The reasons for crossed signals and misunderstandings are numerous and complex. It would be too simple to say that the root of it all lies in the difference between how introverts and extroverts communicate. However, much of the friction – and fiction – that comes from poor communication can be alleviated if we all had a basic understanding of how we each think and speak.

As I've shared before, introverts gain energy from solitude and drain energy from too much social interaction. In contrast, extroverts gain energy from being around and interacting with other people; being alone for too long is tedious and boring.

Another key point of differentiation between these two personality types is how they process information, which in turn influences how they interact with others.

Introverts are internal processors. Their primary source of information and point of reference comes from within themselves. This doesn't mean that are self-absorbed or oblivious to others; they simply rely first and foremost on their inner thoughts to guide them. When an introvert receives information, she takes it in and flips it this way and that in her mind until it's right-side-up enough to be shared with the world.

Extroverts rely more heavily on external stimulus to inform their views and choices. They tend to be verbal processors; rather than spending lots of time in quiet contemplation, they want talk it out. When confronted with a challenge or decision, the extrovert will pull in people for brainstorming or discussion.

Translation, Please.

I know that you believe you understand what you think I said, but I'm not sure you realize that what you heard is not what I meant.
~Robert McCloskey

You probably can see at least one way this difference causes problems in the workplace or at home. Let's consider a common occurrence: an extrovert manager wants to call a team meeting to solve a problem that's just surfaced. Within that team, there are a mixture of introverts and extroverts. The manager decides to have a free-wheeling discussion about the problem and hopes to act immediately after the meeting.

The extroverts dive right in, brainstorming and thinking aloud. There is little to no time lapse between their thought and their speech. Meanwhile, the introverts are taking in the information and turning it over in their minds, thinking through various scenarios and solutions.

Before they even say a word, they may have considered and dismissed several ideas. Rather than talk stream-of-consciousness, they wait until they have a fully formed idea before speaking.

In the meantime, the manager has moved on, the extroverts have all had their say and the meeting comes to an end. The introverts may or may not have gotten to chime in (they prefer not to interrupt; better to ask them what they think), and so several of them choose to have one-on-one conversations with the manager or key people after the meeting.

While the extroverts are like Calvin in the opening quote – leading with speech rather than thoughts – the introverts are like Hobbs and thinking twice.

Put another way, introverts tend to measure twice and cut once.

This can lead to impatience on the part of both personality types. Extroverts want introverts to think and speak up faster; introverts want extroverts to slow down and leave space for more thinking. Without understanding that these tendencies are about as hard-wired as brown eyes or blonde hair, people can go through life thinking introverts are withholding and slow, and extroverts are non-stop blabbermouths.

Closing the Communication Gap

While a zebra can't change its stripes, it can adapt to its environment enough to survive and thrive. Here are a few quick tips to help smooth things out when communication gets a little rocky.

When talking to introverts:

- Give them adequate time to think through a question or problem. If at all possible, don't put them on the spot and demand an immediate answer.

- Offer to provide as much advance information as possible about a situation, and be prepared to patiently answer questions. Introverts like to be prepared and be clear about expectations. Ask if information in writing or verbally is preferred (too much verbal sharing might be overstimulating).

- You may find it's best to intentionally call on introverts in group discussions. Ask, "Do you have anything you'd like to add?" or "Joe, what do you think?" Avoid calling attention to their relative silence with "You're awfully quiet over there." Chances are, the introvert is quiet externally because he's actively listening and forming a response in his head.

- Provide different ways of sharing ideas. Introverts are often more comfortable and do their best thinking through written rather than verbal communication.

- Get comfortable with pauses, longer silences and nonverbal cues. The pace of a conversation with an introvert feels different because she's thinking before she speaks. Once she does start talking, refrain from interrupting or finishing her sentences.

- If you don't know what an introvert is thinking, ask. He may not volunteer the information, simply because it's most comfortable to keep it to himself. Don't compose elaborate stories, make assumptions or read anything into his silence; just ask.

When talking with extroverts:
- Give them time and space to process out-loud, and be patient with the faster energy that they project. This is how they come to conclusions.

Listen carefully, and be willing to interrupt if you need to make a point. Extroverts aren't necessarily going to pause or make room for you. Jump in as needed, and use body language to reinforce your point.

- Understand that extroverts speak first and think later. They may change their mind after some time away from a conversation, so know that's a possibility.

- Be aware that they make decisions based on external feedback, so be ready to be direct and forthcoming. Give feedback in a way that feels comfortable to you and that the extrovert can take it in.

- Ask them what they want to know. Most likely, it's a broad overview or summary of the information, rather than lots of depth or details. Preserve your time and energy by asking what's needed first.

The Last Word

One key to harmonious relationships is understanding and respecting differences in communication style. Without that understanding, we can personalize, make assumptions and completely misinterpret what another person is saying. Patience is critically important, as is allowing space for someone to say "you know, I need time to think about this, and then I'll get back to you" or "it would really help me to be able to talk this through, and you just listen."

When we know what works for us, we can ask for what we want. And sometimes, that's all that's needed to keep bad communication from happening in the first place.

8|Can Being an Introvert Help You Overcome Shyness?

A friend wrote this on my Facebook wall:

"How is shyness different than introversion, especially when you're a solopreneur?"

Great question!

When I first began my journey of serving introverts, I went into research mode. One of the first signs that I had my work cut out for me? When I typed in a search for "introvert" on the photography site iStock.com, they changed the search term to "shy." (When I typed in "extrovert," they switched it to "showing off" ;-))

In most of my presentations, I start by asking the audience to share with one another what adjectives and phrases they associate with "introvert" and "extrovert." Without fail, "shy" is linked to introversion, while "social," "friendly" and "outgoing" are mentioned for extroversion.

The media plays into this definition by linking loners and misanthropic types with introversion. Even the respected journalist Leslie Stahl blurred the lines in a report on "Tech Titans" she did for 60 Minutes. When describing Larry Page, CEO of Google, she shared that he declined to be interviewed for the segment, and that he was known for being "shy, almost introverted."

Her statement sets up introversion as being even further down on the spectrum of social insecurity and aloofness than even shyness.

You'd think we introverts would all be sulking in a corner, afraid, plotting everyone's demise and imaging what life would be like if we were all mute.

Let's start to clear things up with a few definitions...

Shy: 1. not at ease in the company of others 2. easily frightened; timid (1)

Introvert: 1. a shy person. 2. Psychology: a person characterized by concern primarily with his or her own thoughts and feelings (2)

Huh... with these definitions being front and center, it's no wonder there's confusion.

I understand the definition of shy. Being shy is more about social anxiety. You're at the party, and you want to join in the fun, but you're afraid. Overwhelming anxiety keeps you from taking the risk to approach new people or situations. Shyness is a fear-based behavior that can be worked through, if one wants to choose to change it.

The first part of the definition of introvert, on the other hand, is more reflective of what society has imposed on it. We make an assumption that if you don't just jump into the fray and start talking, if you hang around on the edges and look before you leap, that must mean you're a shy introvert (with those two words being interchangeable, joined at the hip).

Can an introvert be shy? Is a shy person possibly an introvert? Yes on both counts. Can an extrovert be shy, reserved or even quiet? Yes to that, too. Shyness can show up for anyone when we're in new situations, we're around people who intimidate us or we don't know what's expected of us.

The second part of the definition above is much more accurate. To expand on it, here's what another source had to say about "introversion":

> A term introduced by the psychologist Carl Jung to describe a person whose motives and actions are directed inward. Introverts tend to be preoccupied with their own thoughts and feelings and minimize their contact with other people. (Compare extrovert.) (3)

When we "minimize contact with other people," we do so because we need to recharge our batteries. We have to dim and mute life for a while so we can function in a bright, noisy world.

In short, you can "get over" or "recover" from being shy.

You don't "get over" or "recover" from being an introvert.

Now that we've looked at the definitions, let's turn to my friend's question and the relationship between introversion, shyness and solopreneurship.

Solopreneurs often encounter the very experiences that can lead to feeling shy: new situations, being around people who intimidate us, not knowing what's expected or what's going to happen next. Do I feel fear around those things sometimes? Heck, yeah!

And my introversion – my ease with solitude and comfort with flying solo – can lead to me to sit alone in that fear a touch longer than the average extrovert might. The fear might show up outwardly as procrastination, perfectionism or withdrawal. It becomes important that I am aware of when I'm going into hibernation mode and letting my introversion enable my fear in an unhealthy way. Instead, I can use my healthy self-awareness to see the fear for what it is and move through it. I can choose to store up my energy through nurturing activities, which gives me the power to feel the fear and do it anyway.

The bottom line need is to recognize the difference between when you're honoring your introversion – taking time for yourself, being an observer, enjoying quiet – and when you're feeling shy or timid.

Dare I say that honoring your introversion can help you overcome your shyness, because you're giving yourself the space and grace to take care of your energy and show up with confidence in those shyness-inducing situations.

You don't have to jump in head-first... you can take your time and mentally prepare. It's all in the spirit of working with your personality, not against it.

References:
(1) Dictionary.com Unabridged. Random House, Inc.
http://dictionary.reference.com/browse/shy

(2) Dictionary.com Unabridged. Random House, Inc.
http://dictionary.reference.com/browse/introverted

(3) Dictionary.com The American Heritage® New Dictionary of Cultural Literacy, Third Edition. Houghton Mifflin Company, 2005.
http://dictionary.reference.com/browse/introverted

Do not feel lonely,
the entire universe
is inside you.

-Rumi

9| Table for One, Please

A few weeks ago, I had a speaking engagement about an hour away from my office. I made plans to meet a friend at a restaurant afterwards. I arrived on time, requested a "table for two" and waited. And waited. And waited.

I was perfectly content passing the time by catching up on news and Facebook on my phone, but I sensed that the server was starting to feel sorry for me. Here I was, alone, waiting for someone who never showed. I finally let her off the hook and said, "I think something must have come up for my friend. I'm going to order some hummus and enjoy the sunshine." (A sunny day in Seattle is not to be missed. And yes, an unexpected event prevented my friend from joining me – it happens.)

I've never had a problem with dining alone, especially if I have something to read. It's actually a pleasant way to recharge, be intentional about enjoying my food, people watch and eavesdrop (shhh!). The only sucky part about dining alone is the greeter who says, "Only one of you today?" while looking at me with upraised eyebrows that hint at pity.

But wait... **There's GOOD NEWS!** No more do I have to be the subject of pity and "oh, so sad to be alone" looks. Thanks to "Invite for a Bite," I never have to eat alone again. According to an April 24, 2012, article on msnbc.msn.com, the newly launched website "helps women who are out and about, be it for business or leisure, connect with other women so they don't get stuck alone at restaurants, pretending to be on the phone or staring longingly at the happy couples around them." (Please see the important **PS following this post)

The article even uses the word "crisis" to describe the undesirable predicament of having to dine solo.

Seriously?

I will acknowledge this: while I have no problem dining alone (or going alone to the movies, a ball game, concert or museum), there are others who don't like it. This provides a nice option for someone who would enjoy a dining companion.

THAT SAID...

The way this service is promoted in the media** highlights our fear of solitude and the stigma around going solo in otherwise social situations. I enjoy eating out with others, and I'm also perfectly content with the pleasure of my own company. At the end of a long day, especially if I'm traveling, the last thing I want to do is expend even more energy talking with a stranger.

And I object to the story's generalization and assumption that there's something wrong with a woman (or man) dining alone. I think rather than coming up with a Band-Aid solution, we should look at the root of it: how we train service professionals (that "Just one?" statement should be the first to go), along with how our society views and (de)values solitude.

Not everything has to be a social experience.

I shared the article on my Facebook Page and within minutes, a flurry of responses appeared. I smiled reading every one of them, enjoying the dialogue of thoughtful, kindred spirits. Here's a sampling of the posts:

For people who want to make new contacts, I think it's a great idea in theory. That said, its very existence perpetuates the stereotypes and stigma.

I'm not the least bit bothered by eating alone and snooty servers can shelve their attitude. I'd be more bothered with having to chat with a stranger.

Obviously depends on your perspective. Some see [dining alone] as a negative; others see it as a positive. I personally find it empowering.

Interesting peek into what is obviously an extrovert's issue – not enough people around to talk to!

I don't know where to start really. As others have said, it perpetuates the stereotype that there is something wrong with dining alone. Maybe they should address why people are so insecure that they can't go out for a meal without feeling like they must be with someone. As for having to sit down and eat with a total stranger as the only option... puhleese.

I like the idea of being able to meet up with someone to share a meal with if that's what I'm in the mood for, but I've always felt sorry for people who "dread" the "table for one" or worry that they're being judged by others because they aren't with someone else. I've dined alone plenty of times in plenty of places and enjoyed myself quite a bit most of those times. It's sad that others don't feel like they have the option of just enjoying themselves.

I can't imagine anybody would feel sorry for me if I eat alone. They ask – "how many," I say "only me" and I smile and I look straight at his eyes and that is it – from that very moment the receptionist doesn't feel sorry for me. Feeling of loneliness or absence of it is in your eyes.

I've never given the slightest thought about what others think, and really, I'm guessing they don't care. Other people aren't paying as much attention as we seem to think. Just can't believe anyone still believes that.

If I shared tips on how to enjoy dining solo, I'd be preaching to the choir. Instead, **here are a few alternatives to "Invite for a Bite" for people (I won't assume only extroverts) who would rather drink hot lava than dine alone:**

View the experience as "Adventures in People Watching." Really notice the people around you, and imagine what might be going on in their lives. Carry a small notebook to capture ideas and impressions that come up... casually, of course. We don't want anyone to think you're a PI or stalker.

Sit at the bar. Several people commented that sitting at the bar was a nice way to be selectively social while still dining alone. If there's no one to talk to, chances are the television will provide adequate distraction, if you want it.

Have a mindful meal. Focus exclusively on the food (whether it's fast food or five star) and notice its texture, smell, color, taste, presentation. Eat slowly and appreciate the experience of nourishing your body. Put away the smart phone and be fully present.

Bring a book, magazine or newspaper to read. This is a tried-and-true introvert default. If you're in a new city, pick up a copy of the local paper or weekly alternative rag. You'll not only get a taste of the local culture, you'll also find events to attend when you have free time.

Visit apps on your phone that you forgot you downloaded. The smart phone (or Kindle/iPad) is the greatest gift to solo diners EVER. For better or worse, it's generally socially acceptable for us to bury our noses in our electronics and ignore our surroundings. If that's your pleasure, mix it up by opening neglected apps. The first time you stumble upon an app you were so excited to download but have never opened since, it'll feel like Christmas morning.

So for those people (or reporters) who see solo diners as sad creatures whose lives would be oh-so-better if they just had a stranger to talk to, hear this: I don't feel stuck being alone, I don't have to call my imaginary friend on the phone, and I don't stare longingly at the happy couples around me. **Most often, I'm a table for one by choice. My ability to enjoy that is something to honor and celebrate.**

** PS: The anti-solo slant might have been journalistic license on the part of the MSNBC reporter, because I don't find the actual "Invite for a Bite" website copy as distasteful. In fact, it almost looks like it could be fun, even for a solo-loving introvert... almost. Get the scoop at http://inviteforabite.com/press

10| 7.5 Reasons I'm Grateful to be an Introvert

Since this is the time of year when we spend time in reflection on the things we're grateful for, I thought I'd turn that idea inward to my own personality.

It may seem silly. After all, wouldn't I naturally be grateful for who I am, for what makes me, me? Not necessarily... since turning my focus to introverts, I've become aware that some people see introversion as something to be changed or fixed, or even as a curse. And there's no reason to judge or negate that feeling; it's a natural reaction to a society that places a higher value (at least on the surface) on extroverted behaviors.

That said, there are lots of reasons to celebrate being an introvert. This is my personal list, to get the celebration started...

1. Depth of Curiosity: I have an intense need to know. This need ranges from the superficial (I had to literally sit on my hands while watching a movie last week, holding myself back from running to IMDb for info) to the profound (shadow work and leadership). Bonus: being curious makes me better at annoying small talk.

2. Ability to be alone: It's impossible to overstate how important this is for me as a solopreneur. I appreciate being able to work for long stretches with only my cats for company. I hadn't thought too much about this until an extrovert friend recently said, "You're lucky you're an introvert, you don't mind working home alone. I'm about to go stir crazy!" Lucky, indeed!

3. Quiet Energy: My energy tends to be a calming presence, which means I don't take up too much space in a room or conversation. And I don't need to take up a lot of space. I have a greater influence when I am intentional and deliberate in my speech and presence.

4. Close Listening: This makes me a good coach. I can listen "in between the words" to what my client is saying, as well as hear what he's saying without thinking about what I'm going to say when he's done talking.

5. Introspection: Since childhood, I've been fascinated with my inner world. I'm grateful for the tangible proof of that fascination: stacks of journals in my closet, chronicling my life from first kiss to marriage.

6. Close Friendships: Growing up, we had astrological plaques in the hallway that gave quick insights to our sign. I'm a Virgo, and I remember two things from my plaque: it said that my "emotions run deep" and that rather than lots of acquaintances, I have a few, close friends. So true. And how I love that. My strong preference for quality over quantity means I've developed a chosen family based on mutual love and respect.

7. Self-Contained: I'm pretty easily amused. It doesn't take much to entertain me; give me a book, a place to nap, my laptop, and I'm generally good to go with very few accessories. This makes me relatively low maintenance and a fairly cheap date :-) .

7.5. Look Before Leaping: This is one of the core traits of an introvert. We like to observe before jumping in. This is a huge asset,

as it keeps us from seriously unintentional actions and big-time goofs.

However, this point is 7.5 for a reason: part of me really appreciates the caution, and part of me really wants to be able to throw caution to the wind just a little bit more. I'm a Recovering Perfectionist... it's hard to leap before looking, because the mess I create could be overwhelming. But the operative word there is "could." Some of the best ideas and breakthroughs come from being willing to make a big stinking mess. My growth edge for 2011 is to trust myself to do more leaping... I'll simply do it the introvert way, with my eyes wide open.

Part Two:

Life as an Introvert Entrepreneur

11| You Miss Every Shot You Don't Take

How long does it take to build a business, or do anything at which you want to be successful?

It depends on how many shots you're willing to take.

My business development action plan includes some activities that are well within familiar territory: Write blog posts and articles. Produce podcasts. Coach clients. Give presentations.

It also includes stuff that feels unfamiliar and a little scary: E-mail and call people **I DON'T ALREADY KNOW**.

Terrifying!

OK, OK, not really "terrifying," but just the idea of it pushes the buttons inside me labeled "insecure and "who are YOU...?"

A conversation with a trusted adviser this morning (one great way to put tape over those buttons, so they can't be pushed so easily) reminded me of this brilliant Wayne Gretzky quote: **"You miss 100% of the shots you don't take."**

So if I don't e-mail, if I don't pick up the phone, then 100% of those people won't learn about how I can help them. They won't have the opportunity to say "tell me more." Instead, **I'm saying "no"**

preemptively, on their behalf.

And why the heck would I want to do that!

When I get too much in my head, or when I start making excuses and deciding it's more important to go match up all my socks, I'll remember: it's really quite easy. All I have to do is show up authentically, believe in and share my value, make an offer and see what happens. **I'm open to outcome, not attached.**

12| Quiet Cultivation: Introverts as Leaders

Bold. Charismatic. Outspoken. Action-Oriented.

For most people, these are often the first words that come up when asked to define a leader. And the more experience we have with leadership, the more we know it's much more complex than that.

The Shifting Face of Leadership

It's been almost 10 years since Jim Collins published his almost instant classic, **"Good to Great." Every chapter has value for businesses of all shapes and sizes, yet one of the findings stands out as particularly important: Level 5 Leadership.**

Why is that one so important? Because it provides concrete evidence that **introverts can be extraordinary leaders.**

The typical introvert does not outwardly match the descriptors I mentioned above. Compared to their extroverted counterparts, they tend to be "seen and not heard" and have a quieter presence in the workplace. Because of this, it's easy to overlook a large part of your employee base when identifying potential leaders.

A Level 5 Leader is characterized by Collins and his team as embodying "a paradoxical mix of personal humility and professional will. They are ambitious, to be sure, but ambitious first and foremost for the company, not themselves."

They also "display compelling modesty, are self-effacing and understated." Other words that describe Level 5 Leaders include quiet, dogged, humble, shy, reserved, modest, gracious, calm, shares or deflects the credit...

Do those words sound familiar?

They should, because **they are often the traits associated with introverts.**

Collins never uses the word "introvert" to describe them; that would be making assumptions about something that is rather complicated. Regardless, his studies show a compelling consistency of introverted traits showing up in Level 5 Leaders.

In fact, he found that those who were more traditionally thought to be CEO material – charismatic, outspoken, ego-centric and self-important – actually did more harm than good to a company. I am NOT going out on a limb to say those folks were all extroverts; that would be a dangerous assumption. It is, however, safe to say that **having a larger-than-life personality does not automatically translate into great leadership.** According to Collins, it's the plow horse – rather than the show horse – that has a more successful track record.

More recent research from 2009 and 2010 has increased awareness about introverts and leadership. Francesca Gino, a Harvard Business School researcher, is advancing the idea that introverts make great leaders. She found that while just 50% of the population demonstrates an extroverted personality, **executive and manager level positions are held disproportionately by extroverts, to the tune of 96%.** She led a team that performed surveys and experiments that highlighted some differences between introvert and extrovert leaders, and how they responded to proactive and passive employees. They found, among other results, that introverts were excellent leaders of proactive employees.

What does this mean for you?

You can grow an organization's culture, teams and leadership pipeline by intentionally reaching out to the quieter crowd. Notice if you or your colleagues exhibit the following traits:

Thoughtfulness: Introverts process internally and generally make a decision and take action only after sufficient consideration. They think before they speak, rather than thinking by speaking.

Calm, Cool, Collected: Because of their thoughtful nature, introverts tend to have a calming energy. This contributes to an atmosphere of trust and safety for others.

Ambition for the company (mission/vision/team), not self: Being front and center, in the spotlight, is not the typical goal of the introvert. Introverts can and do lead the charge, but the focus is always on the company, rather than self-promotion.

Takes responsibility as needed, gives credit when it's due: Their focus on the job at hand means that introverts don't feel a strong need to claim the credit or displace the blame.

Active listening skills: Introverts are keen observers and like to gather information, process it, then come to a conclusion. Most prefer to listen more than talk.

Quiet charisma: Introverted leaders quietly command the respect of those around them and draw people in. Their magnetism is less polarizing and more team-oriented.

Are these traits the exclusive domain of introverts? Absolutely not;

innies and outties can both exhibit these qualities. The point is that **these qualities can be easily overlooked in introverts** who exert their influence behind the scenes and through their more vocal colleagues.

If your efforts at leadership development are slanted towards the more obviously outgoing, social and quick-on-their-feet group, consider this: when it's critical that everyone consider themselves a leader, and everyone contributes to the bottom line, don't you want to be sure that introverts have the same opportunities?

I've heard from many introverts who say that in order to be considered for leadership roles, they pushed themselves to project more extroverted qualities. This certainly expanded their comfort zone, but it also led to less job satisfaction and higher burn-out, since they had to act like someone they weren't in order to be accepted.

As we recognize and acknowledge that strong leadership emerges when an individual can be authentic, we'll experience a wider range of leadership styles that will open everyone up to new possibilities.

References
Gino, Francesca, et.al. (Dec 2010) The Hidden Advantages of Quiet Bosses. *Harvard Business Review*
www.francescagino.com/uploads/4/7/4/7/4747506/grant_gino_hofmann_hbr_2010.pdf

Collins, Jim. (2001) *Good to Great: Why Some Companies Make the Leap... and Others Don't.* Harper Collins.

Do not lose
your inward peace
for anything whatsoever,
even if your whole world
seems upset.

-Saint Francis De Sales

13| 4 Ways to Keep the Lifeblood From Being Sucked Out of You at Events

Hundreds of strangers.

Back-to-back meetings.

Large, impersonal rooms.

Exhibition halls, with vendors smiling behind dishes of chocolate.

Small talk and ice-breakers.

"Optional" happy hours and city tours.

For many introverts, any one of these situations in a day would be draining. **All of them at once? Torture!**

Yet, it's usually these things – and more – that we encounter every time we go to a large event or conference.

I actually love going to conferences and events. Even though the logistics drain me, I enjoy hearing interesting speakers, getting handouts, worksheets and resources, and being challenged to think in new ways. I always figure that if I come away with at least one inspiring idea, paradigm shift or meaningful connection, it was worth the stress and expense of my best energy.

But when I think back to various events I've been to, even the ones I wanted to attend, I had to force myself to go. Just anticipating the event would make me preemptively exhausted. Thank goodness for the conferences that provided a minute-by-minute schedule; I could sit with it each morning and do a mental dress rehearsal, plotting my entrances and exits.

The challenge is that most large events seem to subscribe to the notion that **we have to be together every second of the day**, and cram every minute with activity to get our money's worth. If you want to slip away for some quiet time, you are inevitably going to miss a keynote, a session or a meal, all undesirable options when you've paid good money to be there.

Patty K and I thought we'd put our heads together to brainstorm some ways to help event planners create more introvert-friendly experiences. Patty had the idea after coming back from an event where she talked to several people who said they were overwhelmed and had to drag themselves there, "because I know it'll be good for me." Patty's hunch was that there were lots of introverts out there who wanted to attend events and wanted to have a good experience, but so **many offerings were just downright anti-introvert.**

So to follow up on that hunch, we created a survey. Here are a few insights people shared. The **biggest stresses at large events** include:

- unstructured networking
- little to no opportunity for meaningful connections
- not enough places/opportunities to get away from crowds

- pressure to attend social activities before or after (and in addition to) the regular schedule

When asked what affect these stresses had on the event experience, one respondent wrote, "When I take breaks or leave early, I feel like I'm missing out, even though doing so is crucial to my sanity." Another said, "I usually love them [events] and spend a lot of time with lots of new people (although no parties and annoying exuberance please!), but I'm knackered the week after."

Here are four quick tips that will help make attending your next event a little less stressful, and maybe even fun:

Give yourself permission to leave when you need to leave. Nothing says you have to be present every minute of every event. Often you can get the handouts, a recording or notes from a colleague afterward. They give you a schedule and act like it's do or die, but you have a choice to follow it or not. The alternative is ending the day feeling like you've been run over by a Mac truck... which doesn't exactly support having a positive, energizing experience.

Take on the mental role of host. Plan to focus on making others feel welcome by smiling, asking questions and drawing out those who look uncomfortable. Think of a few stock questions in advance: "What's the best presentation you've been to so far?" or "What did you think of the lunch keynote?" Don't spend lots of energy trying to be dazzling; be fully present, curious and sincere. Own your energy.

Anticipate discomfort. A few things we know for certain: room temperatures fluctuate, food quality is a toss-up, and the availability of scheduled free time is unlikely. Look at the agenda and decide in advance where, if needed, you can go back to your room or go for a walk. Consider the advice from this survey respondent: "Planning REALLY helps, like, bringing a bag with layered clothes, drinks and snacks to events with a packed schedule."

Learn to say "No, thank you." One of the biggest stresses is all of the social extras and obligations that come with being at an event, including (but not limited to) the happy hours, early breakfast meetings and going out with the gang for dinner. While you might feel out-of-the-loop temporarily because you missed hearing the story about the time your boss caught a fish "this big," chances are you'll appreciate your choice to recharge alone much more. Learn to say a firm "No, thanks," and without excuses or being defensive, take care of yourself.

Until that day when planners intentionally make events more introvert friendly (which I'm guessing more than a few extroverts would appreciate as well), we'll just have to take matters into our own hands and do what we can to take care of ourselves.

14| How to Kick Your Paralysis by Analysis Addiction

"KISS: Keep It Simple, Stupid."

All of us, at some point, have probably heard those words spoken to us, or have said them to ourselves.

How rude!

Not the "Keep it simple" part... just the "stupid" part. When we call ourselves or others "stupid" in this context, we're beating ourselves up. It's like a mental "whap" upside the head and a wake-up call to get with the program. (And calling an epiphany a "Duh! moment" – which I did this weekend – isn't particularly compassionate either.)

It's an open acknowledgment of a tendency we all have: to make things much more complicated than they need to be.

After all, it's much more fun – and still leaves room for other addictions, like procrastination, perfection and control – to engage in mental masturbation.

(Oh dear, did I just write that? Yes, I did. Maybe it'll boost my sales!)

Any intelligent fool can make things bigger, more complex, and more violent. It takes a touch of genius – and a lot of courage – to move in the opposite direction. ~E.F. Schumacher

I often wonder if introverts have a special tendency to overindulge in making the simple, complicated. We are internal processors, so the wheels are turning, turning, turning before a thought pops out. We're comfortable spending (draining?) our energy internally. Our thinking happens over time, and what happens when there's too much time? There's enough time for things to get complicated.

We know intellectually that "it's really quite simple," and yet we emotionally get stuck in "there's got to be a better/faster/easier way to do this."

Guess what? Better, faster and easier is usually SIMPLER.

Want to lose weight? Eat less, move more.

Write a book? Butt in seat, fingers on keyboard.

Meditate? Sit down, breathe, be quiet.

Say "no"? Say "no."

Spend less time on Facebook? CLOSE THE TAB.

Build a business? Sit less, show up more.

Is it all that easy? Yes and no. There are more steps, more considerations to each of these desires. The problem is that we get caught up in the steps and considerations, and we forget the bottom line. We think we have to find just the right gym or diet plan… we have to be "in the mood"… we need the perfect sitting cushion… we need to have an excuse before we can say "no"….

Ah, there's the word: Excuse. We blow things out of proportion, elevate their importance to cosmic levels, when if you boil it down to the simple truth, we're making excuses for NOT doing what we want. For NOT succeeding. Because once we succeed, we have to keep doing it again, and again, and again. It's easier to stay stuck in excuses, because our "stupid" gremlins (those powerful negative voices) want to do a happy dance and gleefully sing, "See, I told you so!"

Those gremlins count on us to feed them with regular servings of distractions, diversions and distrust. We think we're doing our due diligence, scrutinizing the situation and considering all possibilities. Instead, we're careening ever closer to paralysis by analysis.

Need an example? This essay. Already, reading over it, I can see that I'm making the idea of simplicity more complicated. I'm trying to explain my position and account for every individual variation and be clever about it and use 20 words when four will do.

You get the point.

Notice: Where am I engaging in mental masturbation?

Ask: What's the simple answer?

Remember: "KISS: Keep It Simple, Superstar!"

It takes courage
to grow up and become
who you really are.

-e.e. cummings

15| The Introvert Entrepreneur or: How I Learned to Stop Worrying & Love the Telephone

There was no more putting it off.

I'd already reorganized my filing system, vacuumed the rug in my office, updated Facebook five times and shredded a stack of old papers and checks from 10 years ago.

It was going to be easy. Really. They'd said "Yes, please contact me."

And yet, I still kept saying, "Oh, I'll start after lunch," and "Just one more e-mail..."

What was it? Why in the world would I be afraid to pick up the phone and call people who had basically given me permission to call them?

When I shared this with a colleague, she sighed heavily and said, "Yes! I know exactly what you mean. What is that about?" And I shared it with my husband Andy when he got home, and he said the same thing. So with at least three of us whose livelihood in part depends on being able to pick up the phone, I'm venturing a guess that we're not alone.

Please tell me we're not alone!

When I asked Andy, "yeah, what IS that about?" he answered from personal experience: It's "call reluctance." It's an aversion to calling someone, a knot-in-the-gut fear that happens when you are about to pick up the phone, or even think about picking up the phone.

As an introvert, my first and preferred communication strategy is e-mail. I hit "send" and cross my fingers that the person will reply in a timely fashion. I think, "please don't make me call you!"

I've had call reluctance most of my life. In professional settings, I used to not be able to make phone calls if anyone was within earshot. I'd script out what I was going to say. It didn't matter if I was making a fundraising call, following up with a prospective client, or simply saying "thank you" to someone and not asking for anything at all.

I flat-out dreaded the phone.

The irony now is not only am I an entrepreneur, but I'm a coach. My primary method of service delivery is on the dreaded phone. So I've learned over time to make friends with the phone. I use Skype and a headset for almost everything, which makes it a more comfortable experience. It enables me to connect more easily with people from around the world, and even saves me an hour on I-5 if I can have virtual coffee with someone.

Let's put it this way: If I didn't learn to love – or at least tolerate – the phone, I wouldn't have a business. Period.

But back to my husband... Andy's personal experience with call reluctance comes from almost 25 years of having an intimate relationship with the phone, first as a telemarketer selling symphony subscriptions, then as a PR director, and now as an executive director (translation: chief fundraiser) for a nonprofit organization. Since he's my resident expert on the subject, I asked him for some tips on how to move through call reluctance. Here's what he shared, mixed in with a few of my own thoughts:

> **Make friends with the phone.** Understand and accept that call reluctance, if you have it, is not going to completely go away. It's an

energy that can be used for good or evil; channel that energy into power and belief in your message, your offerings and your vision.

Remember that it's not about you and your discomfort; making the call is about your business, what's most important to you, your services. Clarify your value proposition and your intention, make the invitation or offer from your heart, and trust that whatever the response is, you can handle it.

Approach your task with curiosity. When you get people on the phone and they're willing to chat, you often will hear and discover things that you wouldn't have through e-mail or even in person. Be open to a conversation that goes beyond your stated purpose.

Get out of your chair. Stand up when you call. Pace around to expend some of that nervous energy. Smile – people can hear a smile when you speak, and it relaxes your voice.

Get dressed for the occasion. If you're a home-based entrepreneur who says you don't do this, you lie: On days when you have no appointments outside the office, you may or may not shower. You may or may not change out of your jammies. You may or may not even brush your teeth in the morning (egads!). To me, it's one of the perks of entrepreneurship. There are days when getting dressed for work involves putting on my sweats and a pair of clean socks. And I've noticed that when I make the effort (it does feel like effort sometimes) to clean up, put on real clothes and take care with my appearance, I am more confident on the phone. I feel more professional and "together," even if no one can see me. Imagine that!

Carve out a time to make the calls. Put it on the calendar, set a timer, and commit yourself to personally reaching out to people. Do nothing else during that time. No Facebook, no Twitter, no e-mail. If it helps, set aside a specific day and time each week for your calls. If you don't have prospect calls, make thank you calls. Pick a time of day when you have the most positive energy. For me, that's the morning, before I have time to psych myself out.

Partner with a call-reluctant friend to hold each other accountable. Set a time for your kick-off call. Each person takes a few minutes to share what calls are important to make. Get your fears out of your system, and share your intention, purpose and desired outcome. Give each other encouragement and support. Agree when you're going to reconnect (maybe 20 or 30 minutes later), then hang up the phone and make the calls. Celebrate with one another when you're done, and acknowledge your mutual success (because no matter what the outcome, making the call makes you successful).

Practice the call before you make it. In other words, visualize success. Take a walk or spend a few minutes in meditation, visualizing and feeling what you want to happen. Imagine the entire scenario, from looking up the person's number, dialing, greeting him when he answers and what you'll say first, all the way to hanging up feeling gratitude for having accomplished your task. Breathe through it and assume a positive outcome.

And speaking of gratitude, **take a moment to say a word of gratitude** for the person you're about to call. Set an intention that your purpose – and your responsibility as an entrepreneur – is to invite that person into something that will make his or her life easier, more successful and more joyful. Allow yourself to feel appreciation for the opportunity to do what you love and share it with others. You have a gift to share. Share it with pride and with a spirit of abundance.

Unless you have Telephonophobia ("the persistent, abnormal, and unwarranted fear of telephones"), you can do this. Give yourself credit each time you make a phone call. Reward yourself. Practice. Take it one call at a time. Be compassionate with yourself.

In time, you might actually begin to enjoy the process of making those calls. You'll see them as an effective, personal way to get your message out and forge relationships, rather than a "to-do" that keeps getting pushed back another day, and another day, and another day.

For me, it's a work in progress. I may never be completely in love with the phone, but I'm committed to shifting my relationship to it in service to my vision and those I want to serve.

16| How to Know When Two Heads Would Be Better Than One

"If you want it done right, do it yourself." *

The words of an introvert, me thinks!

I lived by these words for many years, embracing them wholeheartedly because they gave me permission to fly solo. A co-pilot tended to muck up the works. There was always the possibility of communication challenges, conflicting agendas, and unexpected demands on my precious time and energy.

Introverts and independence go hand-in-hand. It doesn't mean that other people aren't important to us; we simply are more deliberate and even cautious about who we invite into our inner world. We see it very simply: people in, energy out. We can absolutely love and adore those people, and they can still exhaust us. That's why we tend to have intimate circles of friends and place a premium on our alone time.

I've noticed that just as I'm protective of my energy when it comes to personal relationships, I'm almost more protective when it comes to who I bring into my entrepreneurial life. My independent streak and natural curiosity allowed me to be a one-woman show for a while. What

I didn't know, I could figure out...

Until I couldn't figure it out anymore. Until I hit the wall of "OK, I've tried everything I know to do... now what?" And until I realized that some things were too big to tackle on my own, that for the BHAGs** I had, two heads were better than one.

A recent conversation with a professional singer and self-professed introvert reminded me of why we will sometimes do *anything* to find a solution to a challenge, other than ask another person for help.

Vulnerability.

She and I agreed that whenever we bring someone else into our psyche and make the internal external, we are acutely aware of our vulnerability.

> *"There is a crack in everything. That's how the light gets in." Leonard Cohen*

I've always read that beautiful statement with perfectionism in mind. That's certainly one interpretation, but I've also begun seeing it as an invitation to vulnerability. I see it as a call to crack open what I've held so tightly and let the light – other people – in.

How do we introverts invite others into our work in a way that doesn't zap our energy (or cause us to cross the line from cracking open to cracking up)?

Start small. Right now, you may be flying solo with only informal support from friends, family or colleagues. Consider small ways you can start to integrate more formal relationships into your work:

- Join or start a regular Mastermind Group. This brings together a small group of people (less than 10) who are committed to processing through challenges, sharing resources and being mutually supportive. You can learn more about them by doing a web search for "Mastermind Group."

- Enlist an accountability partner for mutual support. My twice-weekly phone calls with my partner are critical to my focus and feeling of connection. We talk in the morning to share our goals and priorities for the day, then check back late in the day to share what went well and where we encountered challenges. This keeps us both on track and helps us avoid the "bright shiny object" syndrome that can distract us from what's most important to accomplish that day.

- One of my coaching clients meets regularly with a friend for a two-hour writing block, during which she writes her weekly blog post. Through this, she experiences a dependable connection and mutual support.

Be strategic. Consider your big picture goals when deciding where it's going to be worth it to stretch your energy by including other people. I have two examples that might spark some ideas for you:

- I formed a "Speaker's Circle," an intimate group of colleagues who share the goal of making public speaking a substantial part of our businesses. We meet bi-monthly to share lessons learned and experiences. In between those conversations, we support each other through referrals, answering "what would you do?" inquiries and cheering each other's wins.

- 2012 is "The Year of The Book." When I think about "BHAGs I have known", this is one that's been on my list for years. My writing skills are solid enough that I could muddle my way through a first draft solo, which seems like an attractive option when I consider the agony of having someone critique my writing. But then I realized it was going to be heavily scrutinized sooner or later, so I might as well enlist a partner early in the process. Enter my book editor, stage left. It's proven to be one of the best strategic partnerships I've ever made. Yes, I still use passive voice too often and ramble on, but she has given me priceless feedback – positive and critical – that not only strengthens my manuscript, but toughens up my sometimes-too-thin skin.

Be proactive. Don't wait until the plane is going down to put on your oxygen mask. There are times when that oxygen mask takes the form of another person providing perspective, encouragement and feedback. Sometimes, because we don't want to bring anyone else down with us, we don't reach out. The situation escalates. We hit bottom. Alone.

Confession time: On occasion, when I'm stressed, I don't even tell my husband what's going on inside my head, even though I trust him more than anyone in the world. He's been 1,000% supportive of my entrepreneurial ventures, but I am loathe to reveal my fears and perceived failures. So I suffer in silence. And hit bottom. Alone. Now that I've noticed this pattern, I'm going to try to open up more. I'm not going to wait until I feel so disconnected from him and everyone else that I can't find my way back.

Who do you have in your life who can help you decompress the stress in progress? If not a spouse, partner or friend, consider working with a professional certified coach. Being able to share both my mistakes and my wins with my coach has made it easier to let others into my business. Our conversations support, affirm and create accountability.

Some people call themselves "soloprenueurs," and by their definition, I would fall into that category. **The reality is that no one, even if you're legally a company of one, is a solopreneur.** We may be independent, and we may be introverts, but we're interconnected. We need each other to succeed. As they say, it takes a village. The key for introverts is to choose that village wisely.

* This proverb has a long history beginning with Miles Coverdale in *Matrymonye* (1541): "That whych thou cannest do conueniently thyselfe commytte it not to another." "If you want a thing well done, do it yourself." ~Charles Spurgeon, *John Ploughman's Pictures*, p. 33 (1880) First cited in the U.S. in *Poems* (1858) by Henry Wadsworth Longfellow. http://forum.quoteland.com/eve/forums/a/tpc/f/99191541/m/786105845 1

** BHAG=Big Hairy Audacious Goal, Jim Collins, "Built to Last"

Start by doing what's
necessary;
then do what's possible;
and suddenly
you are doing the impossible.

-St. Francis of Assisi

17| What the Eiffel Tower Teaches Us About Process

In redoing my home office, I began looking for images for the walls that would inspire and motivate me. This needed to be more than pretty pictures of flowers and landscapes. One day I was in a book store and started sifting through a bin of art prints. Voila! There it was: a series of images of the Eiffel Tower, spanning one year of construction from foundation to finished tower. I'd never had any real interest in the Eiffel Tower and didn't know much beyond that it was built for the World's Fair. Yet, the image spoke to me, and I couldn't wait to get it home and hang it up.

It's really an image to contemplate. For me, it symbolizes the journey and stages of becoming tall, strong and even iconic. I see powerful connections between the Eiffel Tower and process:

The Eiffel Tower didn't spring fully formed out of the ground and instantly become a classic symbol of a city. Sometimes, when I'm feeling discouraged or overwhelmed, I forget that everyone started somewhere. It's easy to think that certain people were just born with their PhD and expert status, in demand on several continents. In reality, they started from the ground and built up. There is no such thing as an "overnight" successes.

The most important growth period happens when it appears that

there is little outside progress. In the case of the Eiffel Tower, the longest period of time between two major points of construction was four months, yet that period exhibits the least amount of change. From the photos, it looks as though that's when critical infrastructure was added that created stability and strength for the remaining upward build. I see this same process with clients. While they are being coached, they are doing a lot of internal building of self-esteem and positive self-talk "infrastructure." They are making huge shifts and changes, ones that form the solid foundation for all future growth.

It takes a village to build something that lasts. The Eiffel Tower had 300+ people involved in its construction. It also has 2.5 million rivets holding it together. Just as the tower needed people who believed in it and solid reinforcements to keep it standing, so do we as individuals on our personal journeys. It's not just about networking; it's about forming relationships of mutual support and trust that will stand the test of time. Just as there's no "overnight success," there are no "self-made millionaires" either. Every successful person has a team of supporters, friends, colleagues and mentors. And when one prospers, they all prosper.

People didn't like the Eiffel Tower at first; they may not like you either. Harsh, I know. When the tower was first constructed, it was assailed with criticism from prominent members of the community as well as the general citizenry. People were actually angry and thought it was an eyesore.

Today, of course, we cannot imagine the Parisian skyline without the Eiffel Tower. Attitudes shifted, and its aesthetic and practical significance (as a communication tower) saved it from the plan to demolish it after 20 years. Paris not long ago celebrated the tower's 120th birthday.

People who succeed in any endeavor often have to persevere through naysayers and wet blankets. They may not like you or your idea. Does that matter? NO. There is plenty of room in your process for people to offer constructive criticism and feedback if it supports your growth. There is no room for those who want to keep you small or who feel threatened.

Surround yourself with people who will build you up, not tear you down. Those who built the tower had to withstand insult and injury. They stood by their vision, and *c'est magnifique*!

18| You Must Be Present to Win: Networking for the Introvert Entrepreneur

This short excerpt is a preview of a chapter from "The Introvert Entrepreneur" by Beth Buelow, to be published in 2013/14.

"I don't like walking into a noisy, crowded room where I don't know anyone."

"Small talk is so challenging. I always feel like I go on and on, and the other person is just looking around the room, trying to escape."

"I feel pressure to sell when I go to a networking event. Otherwise, why go?"

"Networking wears me out, especially those 'happy hour' events that have no structure."

"I'm good at networking with my peers, people who are in the same type of business I'm in. I'm not so good at networking with potential clients or customers."

"Networking has gotten easier for me over the years, but I still feel like it's a necessary evil, rather than something I enjoy."

"I hate networking!"

Do any of those sentiments resonate with you? My guess is that at least one - if not more - of those thoughts have crossed your mind as you go about the business of building your business.

An introvert's natural habitat is one of quiet and solitude or with smaller groups of people. We feel most comfortable and relaxed in an environment that allows for space to think, have meaningful conversations and control how much stimulation is coming our way. For most introverts, networking represents the complete opposite of our natural habitat. Networking events are often noisy, random and awkward... at least, they can feel that way if we're nervous or uncertain how to make ourselves comfortable in an overwhelming environment.

Two things that get in the way of being an effective networker are the stories and beliefs we have about networking: that it's about selling, and that it's full of awkward "what do I do now?" moments, meeting lots of people, small talk and strangers.

Of course, not every networking event is the introvert's definition of hell. There are times when the hell is of our own making, because we decide that it's going to be awful or stressful. We might concoct stories in our heads about being an introvert and therefore being socially awkward. The event itself might be pleasant and even, dare I say it, fun, but we close ourselves down to those possibilities because we've decided in advance that networking is something to be endured, not enjoyed.

Successful networking depends on creating new stories and beliefs that increase our capacity for this important business development activity.

My husband, Andy, taught me one of the most important lessons I'll ever learn about networking. I was in my first job in Milwaukee, working for a very small nonprofit dance company. My recently obtained master's degree prepared me for the technical tasks that had to be done: marketing, fundraising, negotiating contracts, managing a budget. But I was not prepared for the people side of things, and specifically, for networking. Andy, also an introvert, had the very unintrovert job of public relations director at a large arts nonprofit. He had to know how to connect with a wide range of people, from donors to musicians to media. That meant that networking and going to lots of events was important to his work, and since I was married to him, that meant it was important to me, too.

One rainy winter night, he had to make an appearance at an event held by a colleague's agency, celebrating an award they had received. The venue was a bar and, I was sure, going to be full of people talking too loudly and too closely. I literally sat in the car and whined to Andy, "I don't want to go in. I don't know anyone there, it's going to be loud, I'm too tired." I'm sure my voice made it clear that if he made me get out of that car, I was going to make him miserable.

What he said to me next got me out of the car that night, and helps me get out of the car even today. "It's true, you might not know anyone in there. But you might be surprised. And each time you go to one of these events, you'll see one or two or three more people that you know. One day, you'll walk into the room and know half the crowd. That takes time, and you have to start showing up now if that's ever going to happen."

Even 15 years later, I remember and treasure his simple advice. I appreciate it even more now, knowing Andy better and understanding how it's sometimes an effort for him to work up the energy and enthusiasm for yet one more meet and greet. You would never know it seeing him in action. He knows how to connect with people in a way that doesn't completely exhaust him. Watching him, I know that being comfortable with networking is not something you're born with, but is something you can cultivate. Yes, "even if" you're an introvert!

Just as we reframed "failure" in an earlier chapter, we're going to reframe "networking" in such a way that you might actually start inviting more of it into your business development activities. Your business – regardless of whether it's internet-, service- or product-based – depends on you literally or figuratively pounding the pavement, knocking on doors, seeing and being seen. If you have to do it anyway, you might as well find a way to make it less painful and more profitable.

Want to be the first to know when "The Introvert Entrepreneur" is available? Sign up to be on the notification e-mail list at www.TheIntrovertEntrepreneur.com

Part Three:

Miscellanea

19| Weaving in Your Spirit String

About four months ago, I discovered the pleasures of crafting. Give me some paper mache boxes, acrylics, scrapbook paper and Mod Podge, and I'm good to go for at least a few hours. Pretty patterns, smooth paper, intoxicating colors that fill me with delight... until...

Wait... is that an air bubble? Oh shoot, I was silly to think I could free cut a straight line. Did I measure that wrong again? Daggone it, I should have waited for it to dry longer... now I've smudged some of the paper in my enthusiastic effort to rid the surface of air bubbles.

When my perfectionistic tendencies come storming to the surface, they steal some of the delight I was feeling just moments before. I often cast the imperfect item into a bag, saving it for who knows what, because even though it's not perfect, I put my heart and soul into it. I can't possibly toss it.

Now in addition to perfectionism, I've succumbed to attachment. That's a one-two punch that knocks the wind out of me and makes me start to judge whatever I've been working on. Lights out.

The good news is, I've discovered a beautiful way to reframe the perfectionism monster that comes up for all of us, whether we're crafting, creating, working or just plain living.

In the Navajo tradition, rug makers integrate a "spirit string" into their weavings. It's believed that because of the energy the rug makers put into the process, a piece of their spirit or soul gets trapped in the rug as it's woven. The spirit string, a piece of yarn which sticks out slightly from the rug's surface, serves a profound purpose: it allows the very invested soul of the rug maker to escape from the rug.

This idea of weaving in imperfection isn't reserved only for rugs. The Navajo believe that only God is perfect, and that humans cannot match that perfection. So they work in a "mistake" in anything they create, to acknowledge our flawed existence... a spirit string, a misthreaded bead, a catch in the pattern. Often the imperfection is not noticeable and in no way detracts from the object's beauty. Instead, it enhances it.

So now I see those air bubbles and not-quite-exact measurements as my version of spirit strings in my work. Their presence gives me the space and grace to be compassionate with myself and my perfectly imperfect humanity.

The fabric is more colorful and the texture softer when you're motivated by the love of creation rather than the fear of being flawed.

PS: Did you find a typo in this book somewhere? I invite you to see it as a spirit string. My perfectionistic-streak-in-recovery thanks you.

20| Life Lessons from the Lake

There's a phenomenon that happens with many fresh water lakes a few times a year called "lake turnover." Without getting into the details, it's a process that happens when the surface water reaches a certain temperature (39.2 degrees F to be exact) and becomes denser and heavier than the water under it. That top layer sinks and displaces the water below it. This results in "new" water coming to the surface, hence, "turnover." My husband and I witnessed it many times during our years on Grand Traverse Bay in Michigan, and there was something profound about recognizing how naturally and cyclically the lake renewed itself.

The past few weeks have felt like a time of "lake turnover" for me, and I sense that it's happening for others as well. There's an energy in the air of old things, old stories, old assumptions sinking and fading into deep darkness, and newness rising to the surface. And it's not just because the new year is right around the corner. For me, it feels like I've settled into some new truth about myself... like I'm owning who I am more fully. I'm feeling more powerful and confident in my own skin. There's a sensation of new waters rising to the surface, waters that are ready to face the sun and be transformed.

Another word I've been attaching to the sensation is churn. Things are getting stirred up. There's a feeling of anticipation, and more than that, of uncertainty.

I've been listening to Pema Chödrön over the past few weeks. She talks about making friends – or at least, calling a truce – with the uncertainty that we live with every day. We go through phases of collective awareness when we say "these are uncertain times," as if the times before were certain, and we're looking forward to a time when things will be certain again. We're in that place now. We use words like "recovery" and "back to normal," as if there will be a moment when we can all go back to our regularly scheduled programming.

My theory is that we're experiencing the societal equivalent of lake turnover. New energy is coming to the surface, and it's uncomfortable, unpredictable and uncertain. And guess what? It's the new normal. Every day we're creating "normal," choosing what it looks, feels, sounds and tastes like. There's nothing to wait for. We're in it. We're making it happen.

Here's the thing: the turnover, the churn, simply means that it's time to look inward and outward with refreshed eyes, because things are changing. Always. We have an opportunity in every moment to shift from fear to curiosity. There's no use in fighting it. Lake turnover keeps the ecosystem healthy and alive; the turnover that happens in our psyche is no different. Why resist what is natural and necessary?

This moment, right here, is certain. It's what you have to work with.

What are you going to do with it?

The good
and the wise
lead quiet lives.

-Euripides

21| What to Do When You Have a Yucky, Mucky, Sucky Day

There's a fabulous 2003 episode of "Sex and the City" that tells the sad tale of a poorly implemented break-up. Carrie, our lead protagonist, awakes after an evening with her boyfriend to find herself alone with a post-it note that says, "I'm sorry, I can't, don't hate me." She takes the note to breakfast with her gal pals, seething with anger and disgust.

At some point, she decides that the day simply *cannot* go down in history as "the day she got broke up with a post-it." So she and her friends embark on a few adventures (in true NYC, Sex and the City fashion) and finish the day laughing hysterically. In the end, Carrie got her wish: rather than the day being defined by the pathetic post-it break-up, it was transformed into the day she "got arrested for smokin' a doobie."

Yesterday had the potential to be my "post-it day." It's not because someone broke up with me; rather, I received my first official "great proposal, but no thanks" e-mail from a literary agent.

The process of becoming a published author – heck, of putting *anything* original, creative or personal out into the world – is daunting. So is being an entrepreneur. Every day, we're sticking our necks out and hoping someone doesn't chop our heads off. We frequently vacillate between feeling excitement and feeling fear (**two sides of the same coin, really**). We can be excited to put our offerings out there, anticipating the perfect client who is going to be jazzed to find us and say "yes!". We can also experience fear: fear of being judged, rejected, critiqued, ignored.

It feels so incredibly vulnerable to be sending my book idea to potential agents. It's a baring of the soul to strangers who may or may not be safe (we hope they respond kindly, but we also know that some may feel compelled to dish out the harsh truth). The road is long and full of speed bumps, along with an annoying number of "stop," "yield" and "detour" signs.

If we're going to make it through the "nos" to the inevitable "yes," we have to be ready to release attachment to things being just.so. And as corny as it may sound, **we need to know how to graciously receive the lemons and make yummy lemonade.**

That's why I love Carrie's story about the post-it. After I had a mini-tantrum in response to the agent's kind-but-disappointing "thanks but no thanks," I took a big breath and realized: I didn't want this to be the day that I remembered for receiving my first rejection ("I'm sorry, I can't, don't hate me."). I needed it to be remembered for something else, something more positive and promising.

Despite a splitting headache and almost zero motivation, I laced up my running shoes and headed to the gym. It was time for Day 1, Week 1 of the Couch-to-5K program (C25K for short). I'd downloaded the app a few days before and was actually excited to start. The program has numerous advantages that this INFJ loves: structure, solitude and self-pacing. I put on my headphones and released myself into the care of "Allison," who signaled to me when to walk and when to run.

The result? **I found my own personal "reset" button**, and it became "the day I successfully started the C25K program." I was also able to reframe the agent experience into "the day I came one 'no' closer to a 'yes.'"

Whether you're an entrepreneur, artist, writer, leader or underwater basketweaver, you're going to have days that suck. You can love what you do, and you'll still hear "no," experience disappointment and even get royally pissed off. That's all a given.

Here's what I think introverts need to especially consider: We internalize. We process our thoughts beneath the surface, which means that those sucky days can have more power over us. We have the potential to literally stew in our own juices for a long time.

It doesn't have to be that way. I'm all for acknowledging the pain. Let yourself feel it. Wallow for a few minutes, even a few hours. **And realize you don't have to give away your power to the worst thing that happened to you that day.**

You can take it back.

You can redefine your experience.

You have the power to flip the coin from disappointment to excitement.

And that's a coin toss you can win, every time.

22| How to Eat an Elephant

Sometimes I find myself saying the same thing over and over, to myself and to others. This week, it was this piece of wisdom, origin unknown:

How do you eat an elephant? One bite at a time.

It seemed that everyone I talked to this week – clients, friends, family – was experiencing a touch of overwhelm. They had a big goal or project, and it cast a shadow over them that felt dark and ominous. My shadow (actually, my dream) is the book I have in my head that is feeling called to be on paper... and thinking of that shadow as an elephant has me fearing the beast is going to sit right down and squash the life out of me.

Since so many people were in the same boat, I appreciated the reminder that eating an elephant can only be done one way: one bite at a time. Trying to gulp it down in one sitting is asking for severe indigestion.

We know intellectually that the best way to accomplish something big is to approach it in smaller pieces. So why do we run into trouble? Why are we weighed down by the shadow, rather than buoyed by the dream?

Most likely, we have some fear. We have some beliefs about that humongous elephant, and we're by turns motivated and deflated by the sight of it.

The first thing to do is reflect on your relationship to the elephant. Is it YOUR elephant, i.e. is it YOUR goal? Are you working on what you think you "should" be doing, or setting a goal to make others happy? If it's not your elephant, decide how much power you want to give it. What do you have a choice about? Can you decide to release attachment to the goal, knowing you have bigger fish – umm, elephants – to fry?

Let's assume you've determined the elephant is one of your choosing; you've named it Book or Website or Relationship or New Career or Cleaning Out the Garage. How do you feel when you think about being on the other side, accomplished and full? Try renaming the elephant to reflect what you want to experience. Focus on your intention. Using this guidance, my Book elephant might sound like this: I feel empowered and confident as I share my unique voice with the world.

How does that help? By focusing on what I want to feel, I am opening myself to possibility. My elephant might evolve, and if I'm too focused on a specific make and model, appearing at a specific time, I might miss an even better outcome.

> First say to yourself what you would be; and then do what you have to do. ~Epictetus

Some other tips for keeping the elephant in perspective:

Be Authentic: The more "true to you" and authentic your intention and goal, the more likely you are to be committed and take action.

One Bite at a Time: When you feel overwhelmed, it helps to remember to take your commitments and actions and break them into bite size, or fun size, goals. Remind yourself that you have choices about what you say "yes" and "no" to, and when and how you move forward.

Celebrate Your Wins: Each time you reach a milestone, celebrate it! Treat yourself in a way that seems appropriate. Acknowledge your progress and channel that positive energy into taking the next bite.

Enlist Helpers: Surround yourself with people who will support you. They may be friends, colleagues, family members, a coach, mentor or adviser. Keep connected to people who inspire, encourage and challenge you.

Trust the Process: By focusing on the experience you want to have and making choices based on your intention, you can trust that you are moving towards your goal, even if things look differently than you anticipated.

This quote from Francis of Assisi sums up how to eat an elephant: *Start by doing what's necessary; then do what's possible; and suddenly you are doing the impossible.*

Ready to take that first bite?

The most exhausting
thing in life
is being insincere.

-Anne Morrow Lindbergh

23| Why "Fake it 'til you make it" is Lousy Advice

Last week, I attended a workshop about how to create a compelling business vision and purpose. As part of the process, we were asked to name our core values, going so far as to narrow it down to one, unshakable value that we held near and dear.

Even when faced with a long list of lovely words, such as abundance, creativity, excellence, innovation, quality and winning (Ha – I'll never look at that word the same way again – thanks a lot, Mr. Sheen), I found it simple to name my #1 value:

Authenticity.

To be authentic means to be genuine. Trustworthy. Reliable. Truthful.

> *As for butter versus margarine, I trust cows more than chemists.*
> ~Joan Gussow

And with regard to my work with introverts, living in authenticity means honoring your truth. Being who you are, 100%.

This is why the expression "fake it 'til you make it" makes me bristle. I've said those words, and agreed with those words, without really thinking about if they were true. Or even, if they were helpful.

We think that when we're about to do something new, we have to screw up our courage and put on a brave face. The antidote to our fear is to fake it... smile, say that we're excited/happy/optimistic/ready, and then jump. You know, "Just do it."

And we're taught that if you don't feel happy, fake it. Smile, and you'll trick your brain into believing you're happy. I've tried it, and it works for a few minutes. But at least one recent study contradicts that conventional wisdom.

Scientists followed bus drivers over a period of time and compared the moods of those who engaged in "surface acting" (forcing a smile even when unhappy) and "deep acting" (conjuring up happiness from positive thoughts or memories).

The finding? When forcing a smile, "...the subjects' moods deteriorated and they tended to withdraw from work. Trying to suppress negative thoughts, it turns out, may have made those thoughts even more persistent." Conversely, when a subject tapped into positive memories, mood and productivity improved.

When we fake it, we're not acknowledging or honoring our truth. And consider this: if you have to fake it, is that task or feeling a "should"? Is it your choice? Is it in alignment with your values? Is it honoring your personality preferences?

When we fake it, we exhaust ourselves and drain precious energy.

So what do we do when we are facing our fears, or a dreaded task, or trying to climb out of a rut that we feel stuck in, or have to go to the big party that we really don't feel like going to?

First, we intentionally acknowledge that the whole thing feels icky. Scary. Boring. Draining.

Second, we say "AND" (not "but"), and we do what the bus drivers did: we choose to "deep act." We tap into what's already inside us, what's authentic, to pull us through.

This can take the form of feeling gratitude for the adventure or opportunity, or to learn something new.

It can be curiosity, shifting from "I don't know what's going to happen!" to "I wonder what will happen?" (and knowing that whatever happens, you can handle it).

It can be bringing up memories of a big accomplishment, or images of a loved one or your biggest cheerleaders.

> *We are so accustomed to disguise ourselves to others that in the end we become disguised to ourselves.*
> ~François Duc de La Rochefoucauld

Then, when we put on our "game face," we are doing so from a place of authenticity. We've started by being transparent ("This stinks!") and moved to changing our attitude and story, drawing from people, places and things that have heart and meaning for us.

Faking it is tiring for anyone, especially the introvert. We think we have to fake extroversion in order to fit in. In reality, introverts have an extroverted side that can come out to play when we want. Being highly social and outgoing – in our own unique way – doesn't have to be fake.

Think of it this way: your core personality might be introvert, and you have the ability to introvert and extrovert all the time. Those two words are verbs as well as nouns. Part of your own self-discovery and awareness is knowing how you extrovert authentically. Being outgoing, social, gregarious, charismatic... these things are all relative, and they will look different for you than they do for extroverts, or your fellow introverts.

> *If God had wanted me otherwise, He would have created me otherwise.* ~Johann von Goethe

So the next time you think to yourself, "Well, I gotta fake it 'til I make it," stop. Reflect. What's the positive energy within you that's waiting to come to the surface and help you through? Can the smile, the courage, the optimism come from there, rather than being based on falsehoods? Can your natural extroversion – the part that can't wait to share your passion with others – come out to play? How can you balance that with your need to introvert, to recharge?

Faking is a waste of energy, and our energy is one of our most valuable assets. Spend it wisely.

24| How to Stop Thinking and Start Living

I titled this post "How to Stop Thinking and Start Living" not because I had the answer, but because I was hoping you would.

See, I think too much. I live in my head – typical introvert, I think!

It's so bad, I even coined a phrase – while on VACATION, for goodness sakes – "double-think," as in, "I need to double-think on that one a bit."

Really?

Often, thinking "too much" is actually to my benefit. It keeps me from making big goofs, makes me feel prepared, gives me a sense of control, of being thorough.

The downside: it keeps me from making big goofs. We learn from mistakes, don't we? I have a friend who talks about "accelerating your rate of failure." How can I fail, and fail fast, if I'm thinking too much? The faster I fail, the faster I'll succeed.

And all of that feeling prepared, in control stuff? It's really, well, all in my head. It's a false sense of comfort. In reality, I can only think enough to be a reasonable, responsible, thoughtful person. Then other people are going to do what they do, and I can only count on my preparation to keep me grounded, not to have all the answers or to have control over the situation.

What happens when we live too much in our heads? We forget we exist below the neck. Our heart doesn't speak as clearly. Our gut suffers from being ignored. Our hands remain idle. Our feet get stuck in the mud.

We stop feeling and experiencing life first-hand. Everything goes through the fine-mesh filter of our brains, and pragmatism prevails over passion.

A member of The Introvert Entrepreneur Facebook tribe shared, "Sometimes over-thinking can be a retreat FROM feeling, I find, and sometimes an escape from doing, because you have to own what you do and sometimes that's scary."

Another shared, "This morning, I've been thinking (ha!) that I spend so much time thinking, I neglect to simply FEEL."

Well said, friends. As long as a thought is in our heads, we don't have to take responsibility or feel something. It's purely an intellectual exercise.

It's the exposing that thought to the world that's vulnerable. Scary. Risky. Exhilarating. Necessary!

One other tidbit of wisdom a Facebook friend wrote: "Sometimes, done is better than perfect."

Perhaps that's part of the answer... we have to let go of perfection and expectation, and embrace curiosity and vulnerability. Learn to laugh at ourselves. Accelerate our rate of failure so that we increase the chances of success.

Love and honor the thinker in you, TRUST YOURSELF, and don't "double-think" to the point that you get stuck in the mud. You have tremendous gifts to give the world, and they will only come out if they are allowed to move from head to heart to hands.

Here's to living a life of thoughtful action!

I don't hate people;
I just feel better
When they're not around.

-Charles Bukowski

25| Don't Tell Me to "Step Outside My Comfort Zone"

In the world of personal development, the phrase "step outside your comfort zone" (usually proceeded by the words "you have to") shows up so much, I've decided never to use that phrase again.

After all, why would I want to step outside my comfort zone? My comfort zone is filled with **dark chocolate, naps, kitty cats, my BFFs, spending a quiet evening at home and reading in my comfy chair.** It's a cozy place where, according to those who want me to step out of it, I can turn into an indifferent blob of unchallenged humanity, complete with cobwebs and a layer of dust.

Telling me to "step out" of it is telling me to do something scary. I can imagine doing the scary thing, and just like stepping on a hot summer sidewalk with bare feet, I see myself bouncing back over to the cool, comforting grass at the first opportunity.

Since **telling me to "step out" has always felt admonishing** ("get your rear in gear"), I've taken to saying "expand" your comfort zone. Use each new experience to make the circle a little larger, to encompass more experiences. That's felt comfortable. Until now.

What's changed? My realization that the word "comfort" comes with judgment wrapped around it (it is wrapped in my favorite blankie, of course). To most people, *being in the comfort zone = bad/safe, being out = good/scary.*

Now I look at my comfort zone as something I need and want. It's a safe place that recharges me. Maybe it's my introversion coming through loud and clear, but I think my comfort zone is fine just where it is, thank you very much.

Recognizing that there's still a need for an expression that indicates we're growing, I propose stretching our **CAPACITY zone.** I want to expand what I'm capable of doing and being. By using the word capacity, I'm acknowledging that I have certain skills and gifts. It recognizes that I have inherent strengths. I'm perhaps not using them to full capacity, and that's where expansion can happen.

The context shifts: instead of moving from bad/safe to good/scary, I'm moving from good to better. I'm moving from a place of power to expanded power, rather than from weakness to relative power.

How can introverts stretch their Capacity Zone?

Find ways to recharge yourself during large, noisy and/or long events, or when you're with people with faster/higher energy. *Learn to carry your serenity and safety around inside yourself.* It's OK to close your eyes for a minute... step outside for air... take your time in the restroom... wear earplugs. You can increase your capacity for staying in what may be a draining space by developing ways to quickly reconnect with your quieter source of energy.

And while you're at it, *stretch into asking for what you need or want.* When it's time to leave, leave. No excuses, no justifications. If you have something to say, say it. If you can't get a word in edgewise, share it after the conversation. Practice taking care of your needs as you go, rather than letting others talk over or around you. When it comes to your energy and your needs, no one else is going to take care of you.

You have to know – and ask for – what you want.

Make friends with the unknown. Introverts generally like to be prepared and know what to expect. Responding quickly, being put on the spot, dealing with unclear expectations – none of these are natural introvert strengths. Yet, as we know, life is full of situations and people for which we can never be prepared. In those moments, shift from fear to curiosity. Instead of thinking "I don't know what's going to happen!" ask yourself "I wonder what will happen?" Trust that whatever happens, you can handle it.

If you need to build your inner trust, ***take an improv workshop.*** Improv is a safe, structured way to practice managing the unexpected and stretch your capacity zone. There are just enough rules to provide structure and shared expectations, and there is always "permission to fail." Improv is about acceptance, authenticity, being present and trust, all of which also give the introvert a way to create personal energy and safety in the midst of chaos.

The phrase "step outside" or "expand your comfort zone" might speak to some people. It's stopped speaking to me. ***I'm going to start focusing on what I want to grow, building on what I already have, and adding new experiences that expand my capacity.*** As long as there's dark chocolate where I'm going, I'm good.

26| Why I'll Never Say "Just Do It" Ever Again

Of all the marketing slogans in modern times, the phrase "Just Do It" has infiltrated our culture more thoroughly than any other. I'm talking complete assimilation. Like Xerox and Google have become verbs that mean "copy" and "search," "Just Do It" has transcended Nike and is generally used to mean "get off your butt and take action."

And what's wrong with that? Really, I wouldn't be at all surprised if the phrase and what it inspires has **literally saved lives**. In fact, I'm sure it has.

Still, I'm going to make an intentional effort to remove the phrase from my vocabulary. Call me nit-picky, but **one simple word is the undoing** of this widely accepted and unquestioned phrase. The culprit? JUST.

In everyday speech, the word "just" is used to diminish something. *It's just a scratch* (with blood gushing out). *It's just 10 lbs* (that I've been trying to lose for 10 years). *It's just me* (so pay no attention, my presence is not worth noticing). We tell ourselves that it – and we – are not important enough to acknowledge. "Just" is dismissive. In the words

"Just Do It," I hear "Whatever is holding you back isn't worth giving any power or attention. Ignore it."

Saying "just" in this context also hints at frustration. **The phrase "Get over yourself" comes to mind.** We reach a point with ourselves and others when we say "oh, for crying out loud, JUST DO IT." When you put it that way, it's actually *negative* motivation, which I'm fairly certain was not the intention of the phrase founders. "Just Do It" becomes more about moving away from something (pain, frustration, fear) than moving towards something (choice, empowerment, love).

(And I recognize negative or fear-based motivation is exactly what a lot of people respond to; there's a difference between acknowledging the fear and reframing, and allowing the fear to **become** the frame.)

As I've written here before, what we resist, persists. The word "just" might snap me to attention and get me off the couch, but is my new resolve sustainable? Sometimes, yes, if I've done the work. If I haven't, going from "I can't do this" to "Just do it" skips over an examination of my resistance. I'm denying myself a chance to name a fear (usually of not being enough or having enough) and disempower it by acknowledging it and expressing compassion for myself.

Am I being overly dramatic? Over thinking? Jealous that there are probably scads of people who were elevated to the Lifestyles of the Rich & Famous because of three little words, eight common letters?

Perhaps. You may decide I have too much time on my hands and that life's too short to read or write 500+ words about the evils of the word "just." I respect that.

And yet, it's my inquisitive introvert that can't help but find a friend in Socrates: "An unexamined life is not worth living."

I've said "Just Do It" countless times since starting my own business, to myself and my peers. I've only now realized, upon closer examination, that it provides short-term motivation, and it **disowns a natural part of entrepreneurship** (and life): fear.

Believing that a mantra of "Just Do It" is all we need to move through fear is like saying change is as easy as flipping a light switch.

So, **here's what I plan to do**, in addition to excising "Just Do It" from my list of alleged motivators: when that phrase pops into my head, I'm going to take a moment to ask a few questions.

What's in my way?

What's my belief about the "it" I should "just" be doing?

What's important for me to acknowledge and release so I can move forward from love, rather than from frustration or fear?

I offer these questions to you for your consideration. Take what works, leave what doesn't... you won't find me telling you to "Just Do It!"

We do not see things
as they are;
we see things
as we are.

-Anais Nin

27| It Really IS a Conspiracy

I love learning new words. One of the best ones to come along in a while was gifted to me by a colleague and friend: Pronoia. It's the opposite of Paranoia, which is the suspicion that the universe is conspiring against you.

Pronoia is the suspicion the universe is a conspiracy on your behalf. It's the belief that the universe is a friendly place, not one that is harsh and unforgiving.

Think about that: What if the people and situations around us are actually here to support us? What if we approached our lives with the trust that whatever happens is happening perfectly? Would it open us up to see new possibilities, to feeling more calm and confident that we can handle whatever comes our way?

I believe it can. I believe there are instances every day that provide evidence that the forces of the universe are here to help us.

For me, the evidence is in synchronicity.

Synchronicity, as defined by Carl Jung, is a way of describing "meaningful coincidences." This is when you have a thought, and the substance of the thought shows up in reality either exactly with or near the timing of the thought. What makes it meaningful is that it cannot be attributed to mere chance, and the occurrence leads to an insight or affirmation.

As I contemplated Pronoia, I realized that synchronicity is like the universe tapping on our shoulder, reminding us that we're not alone. It's like the universe is asking, "May I have this dance?"

And these moments are all around us, if we take notice. They may not be obvious at the time; fine-tuning our ability to see these meaningful coincidences can start to provide us deeper information about ourselves.

I see synchronicity as evidence that everything is happening perfectly, and that the universe is saying "Hey Beth... I'm here for you. Release! Let me lead." And when I assume the best, rather than the worst, then I can enjoy the benefits of letting Pronoia work its magic.

P.S. The gift of Pronoia was given by Leif Hansen of Spark Interaction. You can learn more about Leif at http://www.SparkInteraction.com

It's not who you are that holds you back; it's who you think you're not.

-Unknown

28| You Know You're an Introvert When...

There are times when I'm talking with people and they'll reveal, "I'm not sure if I'm an introvert or not. I think I might be, but I don't know." Facebook, being the wonderful virtual focus group that it is, became a way to easily present the challenge: "Finish the sentence: You know you're an introvert when..." More than 100 people took up that challenge. They shared a range of feelings and observations that, to them, represented at least one aspect of their introversion.

There were some definite themes: parties, phone calls and unexpected visits received their fair share of mentions. And there were others, some poignant, some surprising, that remind us of the complexity of introverts. As these answers demonstrate, there are as many ways of being an introvert as there are introverts.

And now, on to the list. I wish I could share every contribution here, there were so many wonderful ones. I hope you enjoy these selected insights and find yourself nodding frequently in agreement.

... your way of dealing with anger is writing/typing about what happened and how it made you feel.

... you're glad plans get cancelled!

... your family is getting together today and you're trying to figure out a graceful way to bow out and spend the day alone with a good book instead.

... fuzzy socks+documentaries is more fun than a night out drinking with co-workers.

... at a party, you're more social with the family cat or dog than the people.

... other people equate your silence with snobbishness, conceit or naiveté.

... you escape to the bathroom during a party to recharge your nerves in quiet solitude.

... your Facebook (and other websites) profile picture has your face obscured or your body turned the other way!

... you look forward to the weekends when you have absolutely no plans!

... you would much rather write an e-mail or Facebook message than make a phone call.

... you know that the word "introvert" does not mean the same thing as shy or anti-social.

... you let the phone ring and hope the person calling pays attention to the part of the message that says "the best way to reach me is to send e-mail."

... you love social media and e-mail because it lets you interact with other people on your own terms, back away when you need to, and do it all from your own comfort zone.

... you suddenly realize you haven't left the house for several days.

... you sit alone in your backyard for hours after a long day and watch lightening bugs, perfectly content.

... a significant contributing factor in purchasing a vehicle is that it carries fewer people rather than more people.

... people talk your ear off and then eventually stop to ask, "Why are you so quiet?"

... you wait until the last possible moment to go to the wedding this afternoon with 200 people you actually like, but can't deal with all at once.

... you sit at the kids' table during a party.

... you say to your wife, "I need some 'I' time."

... two minutes or less is a perfect phone call.

... you don't mind cleaning up after someone else's dinner party because there's way less talking and social interaction in the kitchen. A few minutes, semi-alone, to recharge.

... as a kid you were drawing on the chalkboard while all the other Girl Scouts were playing a "getting to know you" game.

... you've given your spouse the car keys just so you could leave the party early.

... you lose track of a conversation while you're having it, because you're too busy thinking about the conversation.

... you long for the days before instant communication.

... you are actually at a party and post a response to this question.

... you answer the phone and you're relieved that it's a wrong number.

... you cobble together yet another odd meal from random stuff left in the pantry so that you can go yet one more day without having to go to the grocery store.

... you listen to others tell their news and forget to tell your own news.

... you're invited to a party but say "no" because you have "other plans" (gardening).

... at a dinner table with 10 other people carrying on four different conversations, you aren't involved in any of them.

... you'd rather spend 20 minutes ordering a pizza online than pick up the phone and get it done in five.

... you stay up super late at night because it's the only time the house is quiet and you can find some time to be all alone... and it's so energizing you can't fall asleep!

... you don't answer the doorbell... even though the curtains are open and the person can see you're home.

... you spend the day not talking to anyone and feel extra energized.

... your idea of a really good time is going to the movies by yourself.

... you sit at home all day reading and tell your spouse you "didn't have time" to do the shopping.

... no one else knows how incredibly witty you are.

... you don't write a response, just read everyone else's.

... all of the comments above feel like they are all yours.

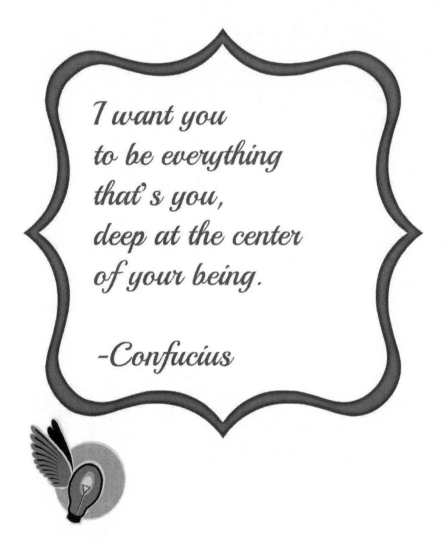

I want you
to be everything
that's you,
deep at the center
of your being.

-Confucius

About the Author

Beth Buelow is known as The Introvert Entrepreneur to a global community of followers and fans. As a certified professional coach and a skilled interviewer, author and speaker, Beth is on a mission to empower introverts to understand, own and leverage their natural strengths. She is certified by the International Coach Federation, and is an active member of the Puget Sound Coaches Association and the Society for Human Resource Management. She is the author of "Insight: Reflections on the Gifts of Being an Introvert" (2012) and "The Introvert Entrepreneur" (coming 2013/14).

Beth has enjoyed sharing her message that "Success is an Inside Job!" with numerous organizations and corporations, including Boeing, Starbucks, Gordon Rees, Xceed Credit Union, Bernston Porter, The Bellevue Club, Puget Sound Business Journal, eWomenNetworking, Ignite Seattle and the King County Chapter of Credit Unions, among others.

She's contributed to blogs and articles in print and online for Psychology Today, Toilet Paper Entrepreneur, Crain's Chicago Business, Seattle Times, The Coaching Commons, Sharp Skirts and Upstart Smart, among others. Her extremely popular podcast, The Introvert Entrepreneur, features interviews with well-known and emerging introvert entrepreneurs, including Susan Cain, Nancy Ancowitz, Laurie Helgoe and Viveka Von Rosen, as well as experts in social media, marketing and sales, personal growth and networking. Beth's individual voice comes out of her experiences as a personal coach, classical musician, arts administrator, nonprofit professional and entrepreneur.

About The Introvert Entrepreneur

The Introvert Entrepreneur was founded in early 2010 as a personal and professional development company that provides services for introverts and those who live, work and play with them. Our goal is to create empowered, productive environments where introverts can flourish. The key to that is understanding and appreciating what it means to be an "innie" in an "outtie" world.

Professional services are designed for entrepreneurs, corporations & organizations and individuals who want to focus on their personal development. Information and inspiration are also provided through a blog, podcast and a variety of social media.

For more information on coaching, training or speaking services, contact:

Beth Buelow, ACC, CPC
www.TheIntrovertEntrepreneur.com
Beth@TheIntrovertEntrepreneur.com
253.617.0779
www.Facebook.com/TheIntrovertEntrepreneur

Coming in 2013/14, "The Introvert Entrepreneur." Want to be the first to know when "The Introvert Entrepreneur" book is available? Sign up to be on the notification e-mail list at www.TheIntrovertEntrepreneur.com

---

Further Reading

The following is a list of selected books about introversion, personality types and Jungian psychology.

You can find all of these books – and more – available for purchase through my Amazon store at **www.IntrovertIslandBooks.com** .

Self-Promotion for Introverts: The Quiet Guide to Getting Ahead
by Nancy Ancowitz

Why Should Extroverts Make All the Money?: Networking Made Easy for the Introvert by Frederica J. Balzano, Marsha Boone Kelly

Gifts Differing: Understanding Personality Type
by Isabel Briggs Myers

Quiet: The Power of Introverts in a World that Can't Stop Talking
by Susan Cain

Splash: An Introvert's Guide to Being Seen, Heard and Remembered
by Carole Cameron

The Introvert's Way: Living a Quiet Life in a Noisy World
by Sophia Dembling

The Successful Introvert: How to Enhance Your Job Search and Advance Your Career by Wendy Gelberg

A Primer of Jungian Psychology by Calvin S. Hall

Introvert Power: Why Your Inner Life Is Your Hidden Strength by Laurie Helgoe

Life Types by Sandra Hirsh & Jean Kummerow

The Portable Jung (Portable Library) by Carl G. Jung

The Introverted Leader: Building on Your Quiet Strength by Jennifer B. Kahnweiler

Please Understand Me: Character and Temperament Types by David Keirsey and Marilyn Bates

Please Understand Me II: Temperament, Character, Intelligence by David Keirsey

Type Talk: The 16 Personality Types That Determine How We Live, Love, and Work by Otto Kroeger and Janet Thuesen

Type Talk at Work by Otto Kroeger with Janet Thuesen and Hile Rutledge

Living Introverted: Learning To Embrace The Quiet Life Without Guilt by Lee Ann Lambert

Introverts in the Church: Finding Our Place in an Extroverted Culture by Adam S. McHugh

Introverts at Ease: An Insider's Guide to a Great Life on Your Terms by Nancy Okerlund

The Introvert Advantage: How to Thrive in an Extrovert World by Marti Olsen Laney

The Introvert and Extrovert in Love: Making It Work When Opposites Attract by Marti Olsen Laney

The Hidden Gifts of the Introverted Child: Helping Your Child Thrive in an Extroverted World by Marti Olsen Laney

Jung to Live by by Eugene Pascal

The Introvert's Guide to Success in Business and Leadership by Lisa Petrilli

Party of One: The Loners' Manifesto by Anneli Rufus

Personality Type: An Owner's Manual by Lenore Thomson

The Happy Introvert: A Wild and Crazy Guide for Celebrating Your True Self by Elizabeth Wagele

Confessions of an Introvert: The Shy Girl's Guide to Career, Networking and Getting the Most Out of Life by Meghan Wier

Networking for People Who Hate Networking: A Field Guide for Introverts, the Overwhelmed, and the Underconnected by Devora Zack

---

Visit www.IntrovertIslandBooks.com for additional resources on personal growth, entrepreneurship and leadership, as well as "Introvert Island" books recommended by guests of "The Introvert Entrepreneur" podcast.

Notes & Insights

Notes & Insights

Notes & Insights

Notes & Insights

Made in the USA
San Bernardino, CA
17 April 2015